Customizing ASP.NET Core 5.0

Turn the right screws in ASP.NET Core to get the most out of the framework

Jürgen Gutsch

BIRMINGHAM—MUMBAI

Customizing ASP.NET Core 5.0

Group Product Manager: Ashwin Nair
Publishing Product Manager: Pavan Ramchandani
Senior Editor: David Sugarman
Content Development Editor: Abhishek Jadhav
Technical Editor: Saurabh Kadave
Copy Editor: Safis Editing
Project Coordinator: Kinjal Bari
Proofreader: Safis Editing
Indexer: Rekha Nair
Production Designer: Jyoti Chauhan

First published: January 2021

Production reference: 1270121

Published by Packt Publishing Ltd.
Livery Place
35 Livery Street
Birmingham
B3 2PB, UK.

ISBN 978-1-80107-786-6

www.packt.com

To my family, friends, colleagues, and the .NET developer community,
who supported and encouraged me to do this work. To my three sons,
who gave me the power to complete it.

– Jürgen Gutsch

Packt.com

Subscribe to our online digital library for full access to over 7,000 books and videos, as well as industry leading tools to help you plan your personal development and advance your career. For more information, please visit our website.

Why subscribe?

- Spend less time learning and more time coding with practical eBooks and Videos from over 4,000 industry professionals

- Improve your learning with Skill Plans built especially for you

- Get a free eBook or video every month

- Fully searchable for easy access to vital information

- Copy and paste, print, and bookmark content

Did you know that Packt offers eBook versions of every book published, with PDF and ePub files available? You can upgrade to the eBook version at packt.com and as a print book customer, you are entitled to a discount on the eBook copy. Get in touch with us at customercare@packtpub.com for more details.

At www.packt.com, you can also read a collection of free technical articles, sign up for a range of free newsletters, and receive exclusive discounts and offers on Packt books and eBooks.

Foreword

I have known Jürgen for more than 7 years and he never ceases to impress me with his knowledge and his experience in software development and web development, his expertise in ASP.NET Core and Azure solutions, and his consultancy and software architecture skills. Jürgen has been involved with ASP.NET since the first releases and has a vast amount of experience with all the .NET and .NET Core versions. His journey has now moved on to Azure and application development in the cloud using the latest ASP.NET Core technologies, Azure DevOps, and cloud-based solutions.

Jürgen is one of the leading community experts in the Swiss and German region and is extremely active in this field. You will always find him present at the local conferences, .NET Core meetups, and Microsoft events, or organizing these events himself. He has been a Microsoft MVP for Developer Technologies since 2015 and I have had the pleasure to develop and learn from him by implementing solutions using some of the early versions and pre-releases of ASP.NET Core or solutions such as ASP.NET Core health checks. He is always helping the .NET community by giving them a chance to speak at meetups and offering speakers a platform. I did my first .NET user group talk in Basel with his help and support.

Above all, he is always there as a friend and I can always ask for support or his help in solving problems and he helps make the .NET community in Switzerland so strong, helpful, and easy for others to join and improve.

Damien Bowden

Blogger on damienbod.com, Microsoft MVP for Developer Technologies, and Senior Software Consultant.
Well known on Twitter as @damien_bod

Contributors

About the author

Jürgen Gutsch is a .NET-addicted web developer from southern Germany. He has been working with .NET and ASP.NET since the early versions in 2002. Before that, he wrote server-side web applications using classic ASP. He is also an active member of the .NET developer community, speaking at conferences and user group events. Jürgen writes for developer magazines; he also publishes articles on his blog and contributes to several open source projects.

Jürgen has been a Microsoft MVP for Developer Technologies since 2015.

He works as a developer, consultant, and trainer for the digital agency YOO Inc. located in Basel (Switzerland). YOO Inc. serves national, as well as international, clients and specializes in creating custom digital solutions for distinct business needs.

You'll find Jürgen on Twitter at @sharpcms.

I want to thank Oli, Kathrin, Marcel, and Maxi for their support and motivation.

About the reviewer

Toi B. Wright has been a Microsoft MVP in ASP.NET for 16 years and is also an ASP Insider. She is an experienced full-stack software developer, book author, courseware author, speaker, and community leader with over 25 years of experience. She has a BS in computer science and engineering from the **Massachusetts Institute of Technology (MIT)** and an MBA from **Carnegie Mellon University (CMU)**.

Packt is searching for authors like you

If you're interested in becoming an author for Packt, please visit `authors.packtpub.com` and apply today. We have worked with thousands of developers and tech professionals, just like you, to help them share their insight with the global tech community. You can make a general application, apply for a specific hot topic that we are recruiting an author for, or submit your own idea.

Table of Contents

4
Configuring and Customizing HTTPS with Kestrel

5
Using IHostedService and BackgroundService

6
Writing Custom Middleware

7
Content Negotiation Using a Custom OutputFormatter

8

Managing Inputs with Custom ModelBinders

9

Creating a Custom ActionFilter

10

Creating Custom TagHelpers

11

Configuring WebHostBuilder

12

Using Different Hosting Models

13

Working with Endpoint Routing

Other Books You May Enjoy

Index

Preface

ASP.NET Core is the most powerful web framework provided by Microsoft and is full of hidden features that make it even more powerful and useful.

Your application should not be made to match the framework; your framework should be able to do what your application really needs. With this book, you will learn how to find the hidden screws you can turn to get the most out of the framework.

Developers working with ASP.NET Core will be able to put their knowledge to work with this practical guide to customizing ASP.NET Core. The book provides a hands-on approach to implementation and its associated methodologies that will have you up and running and productive in no time.

This book is a compact collection of default ASP.NET Core behaviors you might want to change and step-by-step explanations of how to do so.

By the end of this book, you will know how to customize ASP.NET Core to get an optimized application out of it according to your individual needs.

ASP.NET Core architecture overview

To follow the next chapters, you should be familiar with the base architecture of ASP. NET Core and its components. This book tackles almost all of the components of the architecture.

The next figure shows the base architecture overview of ASP.NET Core 5.0. Let's quickly go through the components shown here from the bottom to the top layer:

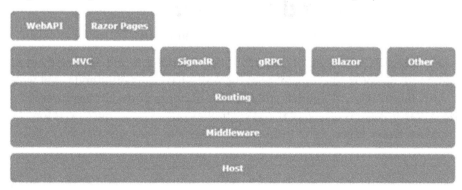

On the bottom, there is the **Hosting** layer. This is the layer that bootstraps the web server and all the stuff that is needed to start up an ASP.NET Core application, including logging, configuration, and the service provider. This layer creates the actual request objects and their dependencies that are used in the layers above.

The next layer above **Hosting** is the **Middleware** layer. This one works with the request object or manipulates it. This attaches the middleware to the request object. It executes the middleware for things such as error handling, authenticating HSTS, CORS, and so on.

Above that, there is the **Routing** layer, which routes the request to the endpoints depending on the route patterns defined. Endpoint routing is the new player from ASP.NET Core 3.1, and separates routing from the UI layers above to enable routing for different endpoints including Blazor, gRPC, and SignalR. As a reminder: in previous versions of ASP.NET Core, routing was part of the MVC layer, and every other UI layer needed to implement its own routing.

The actual endpoints are provided by the fourth layer, the UI layer, which contains the well-known UI frameworks **Blazor**, **gRPC**, **SignalR**, and **MVC**. This is where you will do the most of your work as an ASP.NET Core developer.

Lastly, above **MVC**, you will find **WebAPI** and **Razor Pages**.

What is covered in this book?

This book doesn't cover all the topics mentioned in the architecture overview. This book covers most topics of the hosting layer, because that is the layer that contains the most things you might need to customize. This book tackles middleware and routing, as well as MVC features and some more WebAPI topics, where you can do some magic tricks.

At the beginning of each chapter, we will indicate to which level the topic belongs.

What is not covered and why?

This book doesn't cover Razor Pages, SignalR, gRPC, and Blazor.

The reason is that gRPC and SignalR are already very specialized, and don't really need to be customized. Blazor is a new member of the ASP.NET Core family and is not widely used yet. Also, the author isn't familiar enough with Blazor to know all the screws to customize it. Razor Pages is on top of the MVC framework and customizations for MVC are also valid for Razor Pages.

Who this book is for

This book is for web developers working with ASP.NET Core, who might need to change default behaviors to get things done. The readers should have basic knowledge of ASP. NET Core and C#, since this book does not cover the basics of those technologies. The readers should also have a good knowledge of Visual Studio, Visual Studio Code, or any other code editor that supports ASP.NET Core and C#.

What this book covers

Chapter 1, Customizing Logging, teaches you how to customize the logging behavior and how to add a custom logging provider.

Chapter 2, Customizing App Configuration, helps you understand how to use different configuration sources and add custom configuration providers.

Chapter 3, Customizing Dependency Injection, teaches you how **Dependency Injection** (**DI**) works and how to use a different DI container.

Chapter 4, Configuring and Customizing HTTPS with Kestrel, looks into configuring HTTPS differently.

Chapter 5, Using IHostedService and BackgroundService, makes you understand how to execute tasks in the background.

Chapter 6, Writing Custom Middleware, deals with the HTTP context using middleware.

Chapter 7, Content Negotiation Using a Custom OutputFormatter, teaches you how to output different content types based on the HTTP Accept header.

Chapter 8, Managing Inputs with Custom ModelBinders, helps you create input models with different types of content.

Chapter 9, Creating a Custom ActionFilter, uncovers aspect-oriented programming using ActionFilters.

Chapter 10, Creating Custom TagHelpers, enables you to simplify the UI layer by creating TagHelpers.

Chapter 11, Configuring WebHostBuilder, helps you understand how to set up configuration on the hosting layer.

Chapter 12, Using Different Hosting Models, teaches you about different types of hosting on different platforms.

Chapter 13, Working with Endpoint Routing, helps you understand how to use the new routing to provide custom endpoints.

To get the most out of this book

The readers should have basic knowledge of ASP.NET Core and C#, as well as of Visual Studio, Visual Studio Code, or any other code editor that supports ASP.NET Core and C#.

Software/hardware covered in the book	OS requirements
ASP.NET Core 5.0	Windows, macOS, or any Linux distro

You should install the latest .NET 5 SDK on your machine. Please find the latest version on `https://dotnet.microsoft.com/download/dotnet-core/`.

Feel free to use any code editor you like that supports ASP.NET Core and C#. We recommend using Visual Studio Code (`https://code.visualstudio.com/`), which is available on all platforms and is used by the author of this book.

All the projects in this book will be created using a console, Command Prompt, shell, or PowerShell. Feel free to use whatever console you are comfortable with. The author uses Windows Command Prompt, hosted in the cmder shell (`https://cmder.net/`). We don't recommend using Visual Studio to create the projects, because the basic configuration might change, and the web projects will start on a different port than described in this book.

Are you stuck with .NET Core 3.1? If you are not able to use .NET 5 on your machine for whatever reason, all the samples are also available and work with .NET Core 3.1. The chapters contain comparisons to .NET Core 3.1 whenever there are differences to .NET 5, as version 3.1 is still the current Long-Term Support version of .NET Core.

If you are using the digital version of this book, we advise you to type the code yourself or access the code via the GitHub repository (link available in the next section). Doing so will help you avoid any potential errors related to the copying and pasting of code.

Download the example code files

You can download the example code files for this book from your account at `www.packt.com`. If you purchased this book elsewhere, you can visit `www.packtpub.com/support` and register to have the files emailed directly to you.

You can download the code files by following these steps:

1. Log in or register at www.packt.com.

2. Select the **Support** tab.

3. Click on **Code Downloads**.

4. Enter the name of the book in the **Search** box and follow the onscreen instructions.

Once the file is downloaded, please make sure that you unzip or extract the folder using the latest version of:

- WinRAR/7-Zip for Windows

- Zipeg/iZip/UnRarX for Mac

- 7-Zip/PeaZip for Linux

The code bundle for the book is also hosted on GitHub at https://github.com/ PacktPublishing/Customizing-ASP.NET-Core-5.0. In case there's an update to the code, it will be updated on the existing GitHub repository.

We also have other code bundles from our rich catalog of books and videos available at https://github.com/PacktPublishing/. Check them out!

Conventions used

There are a number of text conventions used throughout this book.

Code in text: Indicates code words in text, database table names, folder names, filenames, file extensions, pathnames, dummy URLs, user input, and Twitter handles. Here is an example: "Open the file Startup.cs of the project you just created."

A block of code is set as follows:

```
public Task StopAsync(CancellationToken cancellationToken)
{
    logger.LogInformation("Hosted service stopping");
    return Task.CompletedTask;
}
```

When we wish to draw your attention to a particular part of a code block, the relevant lines or items are set in bold:

```
app.UseEndpoints(endpoints =>
{
    endpoints.MapGet("/", async context =>
    {
        await context.Response.WriteAsync(
            "Hello World!");
    });

    endpoints.MapAppStatus("/status", "Status");
});
```

Any command-line input or output is written as follows:

```
dotnet new web -n SampleProject -o SampleProject
cd SampleProject
code .
```

Bold: Indicates a new term, an important word, or words that you see onscreen. For example, words in menus or dialog boxes appear in the text like this. Here is an example: "Select **System info** from the **Administration** panel."

> **Tips or important notes**
> Appear like this.

Get in touch

Feedback from our readers is always welcome.

General feedback: If you have questions about any aspect of this book, mention the book title in the subject of your message and email us at customercare@packtpub.com.

Errata: Although we have taken every care to ensure the accuracy of our content, mistakes do happen. If you have found a mistake in this book, we would be grateful if you would report this to us. Please visit www.packtpub.com/support/errata, selecting your book, clicking on the Errata Submission Form link, and entering the details.

Piracy: If you come across any illegal copies of our works in any form on the Internet, we would be grateful if you would provide us with the location address or website name. Please contact us at copyright@packt.com with a link to the material.

If you are interested in becoming an author: If there is a topic that you have expertise in and you are interested in either writing or contributing to a book, please visit authors.packtpub.com.

Reviews

Please leave a review. Once you have read and used this book, why not leave a review on the site that you purchased it from? Potential readers can then see and use your unbiased opinion to make purchase decisions, we at Packt can understand what you think about our products, and our authors can see your feedback on their book. Thank you!

For more information about Packt, please visit packt.com.

1
Customizing Logging

In this first chapter of the book about customizing ASP.NET Core, you will see how to customize logging. The default logging only writes to the console or to the debug window. This is quite good for the majority of cases, but it may be the case that you need to log to a sink, such as a file or a database. Perhaps you want to extend the logger with additional information. In these cases, you need to know how to change the default logging.

In this chapter, we will be covering the following topics:

- Configuring logging
- Creating a custom logger
- Plugging in an existing third-party logger provider

The topics in this chapter refer to the hosting layer of the ASP.NET Core architecture:

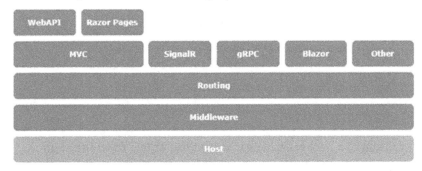

Figure 1.1 – ASP.NET Core architecture

Technical requirements

To follow the descriptions in this chapter, you will need to create an ASP.NET Core MVC application. Open your console, shell, or bash terminal, and change to your working directory. Use the following command to create a new MVC application:

```
dotnet new mvc -n LoggingSample -o LoggingSample
```

Now, open the project in Visual Studio by double-clicking the project file or, in VS Code, by typing the following command in the already open console:

```
cd LoggingSample
code.
```

All of the code samples in this chapter can be found in the GitHub repository for this book at https://github.com/PacktPublishing/Customizing-ASP.NET-Core-5.0/tree/main/Chapter01.

Configuring logging

In previous versions of ASP.NET Core (pre-2.0), logging was configured in Startup.cs. As a reminder, since version 2.0, the Startup.cs file has been simplified, and a lot of configurations were moved to default WebHostBuilder, which is called in Program.cs. Also, logging was moved to default WebHostBuilder.

In ASP.NET Core 3.1 and later versions, the Program.cs file gets more generic, and IHostBuilder will be created first. IHostBuilder is pretty useful for bootstrapping an application without all the ASP.NET web stuff. We'll learn a lot more about IHostBuilder later on in the following chapters. With this IHostBuilder, we create IWebHostBuilder to configure ASP.NET Core. In ASP.NET Core 3.1 and later versions, we get IWebHostBuilder with the webBuilder variable:

```
public class Program
{
    public static void Main(string[] args)
    {
        CreateHostBuilder(args).Build().Run();
    }

    public static IHostBuilder CreateHostBuilder(string[]
        args) =>
```

```
    Host.CreateDefaultBuilder(args)
        .ConfigureWebHostDefaults(webBuilder =>
        {
            webBuilder.UseStartup<Startup>();
        });
}
```

In ASP.NET Core, you are able to override and customize almost everything. This includes logging. IWebHostBuilder has a lot of extension methods to override the default behavior. To override the default settings for logging, we need to choose the ConfigureLogging method. The following code snippet shows almost exactly the same logging as was configured inside the ConfigureWebHostDefaults() method:

```
Host.CreateDefaultBuilder(args)
    .ConfigureWebHostDefaults(webBuilder =>
    {
        webBuilder
            .ConfigureLogging((hostingContext, logging) =>
            {
                logging.AddConfiguration(
                    hostingContext.Configuration.GetSection
                        ("Logging"));
                logging.AddConsole();
                logging.AddDebug();
            })
            .UseStartup<Startup>();
    });
```

This method needs a lambda that gets WebHostBuilderContext and LoggingBuilder to configure logging.

Now that we've seen how to configure logging, let's look at building a custom logger.

Creating a custom logger

To demonstrate a custom logger, let's use a small simple logger I created that is able to colorize log entries with a specific log level in the console. This is called `ColoredConsoleLogger` and will be added and created using `LoggerProvider`, which we also need to write for ourselves. To specify the color and the log level to colorize, we need to add a configuration class.

In the next snippets, all three parts (`Logger`, `LoggerProvider`, and `Configuration`) are shown:

1. Let's create the configuration class of our logger. We will call it `ColoredConsoleLoggerConfiguration`. This class contains three properties to define – `LogLevel`, `EventId`, and `Color` that can be set:

    ```
    public class ColoredConsoleLoggerConfiguration
    {
        public LogLevel LogLevel { get; set; } =
          LogLevel.Warning;
        public int EventId { get; set; } = 0;
        public ConsoleColor Color { get; set; } =
          ConsoleColor.Yellow;
    }
    ```

2. Next, we need a provider to retrieve the configuration and create the actual logger instance:

    ```
    public class ColoredConsoleLoggerProvider :
      IloggerProvider
    {
        private readonly ColoredConsoleLoggerConfiguration
          _config;
        private readonly ConcurrentDictionary<string,
          ColoredConsoleLogger> _loggers =
            new ConcurrentDictionary<string,
              ColoredConsoleLogger>();

        public ColoredConsoleLoggerProvider
          (ColoredConsoleLoggerConfiguration config)
        {
    ```

```
        _config = config;
    }

    public ILogger CreateLogger(string categoryName)
    {
        return _loggers.GetOrAdd(categoryName, name =>
            new ColoredConsoleLogger(name, _config));
    }

    public void Dispose()
    {
        _loggers.Clear();
    }
}
```

3. The third class is the actual logger we want to use:

```
public class ColoredConsoleLogger : Ilogger
{
    private static object _lock = new Object();
    private readonly string _name;
    private readonly ColoredConsoleLoggerConfiguration
      _config;

    public ColoredConsoleLogger(
        string name,
        ColoredConsoleLoggerConfiguration config)
    {
        _name = name;
        _config = config;
    }

    public IDisposable BeginScope<TState>(TState
      state)
    {
        return null;
    }
```

```csharp
public bool IsEnabled(LogLevel logLevel)
{
    return logLevel == _config.LogLevel;
}


public void Log<TState>(
    LogLevel logLevel,
    EventId eventId,
    TState state,
    Exception exception,
    Func<TState, Exception, string> formatter)
{
    if (!IsEnabled(logLevel))
    {
        return;
    }

    lock (_lock)
    {
        if (_config.EventId == 0 ||
          _config.EventId
          == eventId.Id)
        {
            var color = Console.ForegroundColor;
            Console.ForegroundColor =
              _config.Color;

            Console.WriteLine($"{logLevel.ToString()}
                - {eventId.Id} - {_name} -
                {formatter(state, exception)}");
            Console.ForegroundColor = color;
        }
    }
}
```

We now need to lock the actual console output, because we will encounter some race conditions where incorrect log entries get colored with the wrong color because the console itself is not really thread safe.

4.   If this is done, we can start to plug in the new logger to the configuration in the `Program.cs` file:

```
logging.ClearProviders();
var config = new ColoredConsoleLoggerConfiguration
{
    LogLevel = LogLevel.Information,
    Color = ConsoleColor.Red
};
logging.AddProvider(new
    ColoredConsoleLoggerProvider(config));
```

In case you don't want to use the existing loggers, you can clear all the logger providers added previously. Then, we call `AddProvider` to add a new instance of our `ColoredConsoleLoggerProvider` class with the specific settings. We could also add some more instances of the provider with different settings.

This shows how you could handle different log levels in a different way. You could use this to send emails regarding hard errors, to log debug messages to a different log sink from regular informational messages, and so on:

```
C:\git\dotnetconf\001-logging\LoggingSample
λ dotnet run
Using launch settings from C:\git\dotnetconf\001-logging\LoggingSample\Properties\la
unchSettings.json...
Information - 0 - Microsoft.AspNetCore.DataProtection.KeyManagement.XmlKeyManager -
User profile is available. Using 'C:\Users\Juergen\AppData\Local\ASP.NET\DataProtect
ion-Keys' as key repository and Windows DPAPI to encrypt keys at rest.
Hosting environment: Development
Content root path: C:\git\dotnetconf\001-logging\LoggingSample
Now listening on: https://localhost:5001
Now listening on: http://localhost:5000
Application started. Press Ctrl+C to shut down.
```

Figure 1.2 – A screenshot of the custom logger

Figure 1.2 shows the colored output of the previously created custom logger.

In many cases, it doesn't make sense to write a custom logger because many good third-party loggers are already available, such as ELMAH, log4net, and NLog. In the next section, we will see how to use NLog in ASP.NET Core.

Plugging in an existing third-party logger provider

NLog was one of the very first loggers that was available as a .NET Standard library and usable in ASP.NET Core. NLog also already provides a logger provider to easily plug into ASP.NET Core.

You will find NLog via NuGet (`https://www.nuget.org/packages/NLog.Web.AspNetCore`) and on GitHub (`https://github.com/NLog/NLog.Web`). Even if NLog is not yet explicitly available for ASP.NET Core 5.0, it will nevertheless work with this version:

1. We need to add an `NLog.Config` file that defines two different sinks to log all messages in a single log file, and custom messages only in another file. Since this file is too long to print, you can view it or download it directly from GitHub: `https://github.com/PacktPublishing/Customizing-ASP.NET-Core-5.0/blob/main/Chapter01/LoggingSample5.0/NLog.Config`.

2. We then need to add the NLog ASP.NET Core package from NuGet:

    ```
    dotnet add package NLog.Web.AspNetCore
    ```

    > **Important note**
    > Be sure that you are in the project directory before you execute that command!

3. Now, you only need to clear all the other providers in the `ConfigureLogging` method in `Program.cs` and to use `NLog` with the `IWebHostBuilder` using the `UseNLog()` method:

    ```
    Host.CreateDefaultBuilder(args)
        .ConfigureWebHostDefaults(webBuilder =>
        {
            webBuilder
                .ConfigureLogging((hostingContext,
                    logging)
                    =>
                {
                    logging.ClearProviders();
    ```

```
                logging.SetMinimumLevel(LogLevel.Trace);
            })
        .UseNLog()
        .UseStartup<Startup>();
    });
```

Here, you can add as many logger providers as you require.

That covers using an existing logger. Let's now recap what we've covered in these initial pages.

Summary

The good thing about hiding the basic configuration is that it allows you to clean up the newly scaffolded projects and to keep the actual start as simple as possible. The developer is able to focus on the actual features. However, the more the application grows, the more important logging becomes. The default logging configuration is easy and it works like a charm, but in production you need a persisted log to see errors from the past. Therefore, you need to add a custom logging or a more flexible logger, such as NLog or log4net.

You will learn more about how to configure ASP.NET Core in the next chapter.

2
Customizing App Configuration

This second chapter is about application configuration, how to use it, and how to customize the ASP.NET configuration to employ different ways to configure your app. Perhaps you already have an existing XML configuration, or want to share a YAML configuration file over different kinds of applications. Sometimes, it also makes sense to read configuration values out of a database.

In this chapter, we will be covering the following topics:

- Configuring the configuration
- Using typed configurations
- Configuration using INI files
- Configuration providers

The topics in this chapter refer to the hosting layer of the ASP.NET Core architecture:

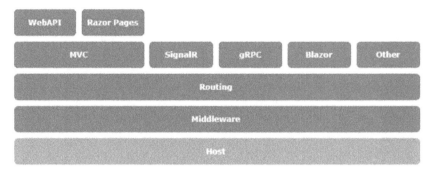

Figure 2.1 – ASP.NET Core architecture

Technical requirements

To follow the descriptions in this chapter, you will need to create an ASP.NET Core MVC application. Open your console, shell, or bash terminal, and change to your working directory. Use the following command to create a new MVC application:

```
dotnet new mvc -n ConfigureSample -o ConfigureSample
```

Now, open the project in Visual Studio by double-clicking the project file or, in VS Code, by typing the following command in the already open console:

```
cd ConfigureSample
code .
```

All of the code samples in this chapter can be found in the GitHub repository for this book at https://github.com/PacktPublishing/Customizing-ASP. NET-Core-5.0/tree/main/Chapter02.

Configuring the configuration

Let's start by looking at how to configure your various configuration options.

Since ASP.NET Core 2.0, the configuration is hidden in the default configuration of WebHostBuilder, and no longer part of Startup.cs. This helps to keep the startup clean and simple.

In ASP.NET Core 3.1 and ASP.NET Core 5.0, the code looks like this:

```
// ASP.NET Core 3.0 and later
public class Program
{
    public static void Main(string[] args)
    {
        CreateWebHostBuilder(args).Build().Run();
    }

    public static IHostBuilder CreateHostBuilder(string[]
      args) =>
        Host.CreateDefaultBuilder(args)
            .ConfigureWebHostDefaults(webBuilder =>
            {
                webBuilder.UseStartup<Startup>();
            }
}
```

Fortunately, you are also able to override the default settings to customize the configuration in a way you need it.

When you create a new ASP.NET Core project, you will already have `appsettings.json` and `appsettings.Development.json` configured. You can, and should, use these configuration files to configure your app; this is the pre-configured way, and most ASP.NET Core developers will look for an `appsettings.json` file to configure the application. This is absolutely fine and works pretty well.

The following code snippet shows the encapsulated default configuration to read the `appsettings.json` files:

```
Host.CreateDefaultBuilder(args)
    .ConfigureWebHostDefaults(webBuilder =>
    {
        webBuilder
          .ConfigureAppConfiguration((builderContext,
            config) =>
        {
            var env = builderContext.HostingEnvironment;
```

```
        config.SetBasePath(env.ContentRootPath);
        config.AddJsonFile(
            "appsettings.json",
            optional: false,
            reloadOnChange: true);
        config.AddJsonFile(
            $"appsettings.{env.EnvironmentName}.json",
            optional: true,
            reloadOnChange: true);

        config.AddEnvironmentVariables();
    })
    .UseStartup<Startup>();
});
```

This configuration also sets the base path of the application and adds the configuration via environment variables. The `ConfigureAppConfiguration` method accepts a lambda method that gets `WebHostBuilderContext` and `ConfigurationBuilder` passed in.

Whenever you customize the application configuration, you should add the configuration via environment variables as a final step, using the `AddEnvironmentVariables()` method. The order of the configuration matters, and the configuration providers that you add later on will override the configurations added previously. Be sure that the environment variables always override the configurations that are set via a file. This way, you also ensure that the configuration of your application on an Azure App Service will be passed to the application as environment variables.

`IConfigurationBuilder` has a lot of extension methods to add more configurations, such as XML or INI configuration files, and in-memory configurations. You can find additional configuration providers built by the community to read in YAML files, database values, and a lot more. In an upcoming section, we will see how to read INI files. First, we will look at using typed configurations.

Using typed configurations

Before trying to read INI files, it makes sense for you to see how to use typed configurations instead of reading the configuration via `IConfiguration`, key by key.

To read a typed configuration, you need to define the type to configure. I usually create a class called `AppSettings`, as follows:

```
public class AppSettings
{
    public int Foo { get; set; }
    public string Bar { get; set; }
}
```

This is a simple POCO class that will only contain the application setting values. These classes can then be filled with specific configuration sections inside the `ConfigureServices` method in `Startup.cs`:

```
services.Configure<AppSettings>
    (Configuration.GetSection("AppSettings"));
```

This way, the typed configuration also gets registered as a service in the dependency injection container and can be used everywhere in the application. You are able to create different configuration types for each configuration section. In most cases, one section should be fine, but sometimes it makes sense to divide the settings into different sections. The next snippet shows how to use the configuration in an MVC controller:

```
public class HomeController : Controller
{
    private readonly AppSettings _options;

    public HomeController(IOptions<AppSettings> options)
    {
        _options = options.Value;
    }
```

`IOptions<AppSettings>` is a wrapper around our `AppSettings` type, and the `Value` property contains the actual instance of `AppSettings`, including the values from the configuration file.

To try that, the `appsettings.json` file needs to have the `AppSettings` section configured, otherwise the values are null or not set. Let's now add the section to `appsettings.json`:

```
{
    "Logging": {
```

```
        "LogLevel": {
            "Default": "Warning"
        }
    },
    "AllowedHosts": "*",
    "AppSettings": {
        "Foo": 123,
        "Bar": "Bar"
    }
}
```

Next, we'll examine how INI files can be used for configuration.

Configuration using INI files

To also use INI files to configure the application, you will need to add the INI configuration inside the `ConfigureAppConfiguration()` method in `Program.cs`:

```
config.AddIniFile(
    "appsettings.ini",
    optional: false,
    reloadOnChange: true);
config.AddJsonFile(
    $"appsettings.{env.EnvironmentName}.ini",
    optional: true,
    reloadOnChange: true);
```

This code loads the INI files the same way as the JSON configuration files. The first line is a required configuration, and the second line is an optional configuration depending on the current runtime environment.

The INI file could look like this:

```
[AppSettings]
Bar="FooBar"
```

As you can see, this file contains a section called `AppSettings` and a property called `Bar`.

Earlier, we said that the order of the configuration matters. If you add the two lines to configure via INI files after the configuration via JSON files, the INI files will override the settings from the JSON files. The `Bar` property gets overridden with `"FooBar"` and the `Foo` property stays the same, because it will not be overridden. Also, the values out of the INI file will be available via the typed configuration created previously.

Every other configuration provider will work the same way. Let's now see how a configuration provider will look.

Configuration providers

A configuration provider is an implementation of `IConfigurationProvider` that is created by a configuration source, which is an implementation of `IConfigurationSource`. The configuration provider then reads the data from somewhere and provides it via `Dictionary`.

To add a custom or third-party configuration provider to ASP.NET Core, you will need to call the `Add` method on `ConfigurationBuilder` and insert the configuration source. This is just an example:

```
Host.CreateDefaultBuilder(args)
    .ConfigureWebHostDefaults(webBuilder =>
    {

        webBuilder.ConfigureAppConfiguration((builderContext,
           config) =>
           {
               var env = builderContext.HostingEnvironment;
               config.SetBasePath(env.ContentRootPath);
               config.AddJsonFile(
                   "appsettings.json",
                   optional: false,
                   reloadOnChange: true);
               config.AddJsonFile(
                   $"appsettings.{env.EnvironmentName}.json",
                   optional: true,
                   reloadOnChange: true);

               // add new configuration source
```

```
        config.Add(new MyCustomConfigurationSource
        {
            SourceConfig = //configure whatever source
            Optional = false,
            ReloadOnChange = true
        });

        config.AddEnvironmentVariables();
    })
    .UseStartup<Startup>();
});
```

Usually, you would create an extension method to add the configuration source more easily:

```
config.AddMyCustomSource("source", optional: false,
    reloadOnChange: true);
```

A really detailed concrete example about how to create a custom configuration provider has been written by Andrew Lock. You can find this in the *Further reading* section of this chapter.

Summary

In most cases, you will not need to add a different configuration provider or to create your own configuration provider, but it's good to know how to change it, just in case. Also, using typed configuration is a nice way to read and provide the settings. In classic ASP.NET, we used a manually created façade to read the application settings in a typed manner. Now, this is automatically done by just providing a type. This type will be automatically instantiated, filled, and provided, via a dependency injection.

To learn more about customizing dependency injection in ASP.NET Core 5.0, let's have a look at the next chapter.

Further reading

Andrew Lock, Creating a custom ConfiguationProvider in ASP.NET Core: https://andrewlock.net/creating-a-custom-iconfigurationprovider-in-asp-net-core-to-parse-yaml/.

3
Customizing Dependency Injection

In this third chapter, we'll take a look at ASP.NET Core **dependency injection** and how to customize it to use a different dependency injection container, if needed.

In this chapter, we will be covering the following topics:

- Using a different dependency injection container
- Looking at the `ConfigureServices` method
- Using a different `ServiceProvider` type
- Introducing Scrutor

The topics in this chapter refer to the hosting layer of the ASP.NET Core architecture:

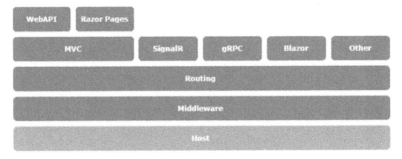

Figure 3.1 – ASP.NET Core architecture

Technical requirements

To follow the descriptions in this chapter, you will need to create an ASP.NET Core MVC application. Open your console, shell, or bash terminal, and change to your working directory. Use the following command to create a new MVC application:

```
dotnet new mvc -n DiSample -o DiSample
```

Now, open the project in Visual Studio by double-clicking the project file or, in VS Code, by typing the following command in the already open console:

```
cd DiSample
code .
```

All of the code samples in this chapter can be found in the GitHub repository for this book at https://github.com/PacktPublishing/Customizing-ASP.NET-Core-5.0/tree/main/Chapter03.

Using a different dependency injection container

In most projects, you don't really need to use a different **dependency injection (DI)** container. The existing DI implementation in ASP.NET Core supports the main basic features and works both effectively and quickly. However, some other DI containers support a number of interesting features you might want to use in your application:

- **Ninject** allows you to create an application that supports modules as lightweight dependencies; for example, modules you might want to put into a specific directory and have them be automatically registered in your application.

- You might want to configure the services in a configuration file outside the application, in an XML or JSON file instead of in C# only. This is a common feature in various DI containers, but not yet supported in ASP.NET Core.

- Perhaps you don't want to have an immutable DI container because you want to add services at runtime. This is also a common feature in some DI containers.

Let's now see how the `ConfigureServices` method enables you to use alternative DI containers.

Looking at the ConfigureServices method

Let's compare the current `ConfigureServices` method with a previous Long-Term Support version to see what has changed. If you were to create a new ASP.NET Core project using version 3.1 and open `Startup.cs`, you would find the method to configure the services, which looks like this:

```
public void ConfigureServices(IServiceCollection services)
{
    services.Configure<CookiePolicyOptions>(options =>
    {
        // This lambda determines whether user
        // consent for non-essential cookies is
        // needed for a given request.
        options.CheckConsentNeeded = context => true;
    });

    services.AddControllersWithViews();
    services.AddRazorPages();
}
```

In contrast, in ASP.NET Core 5.0, it looks like this:

```
public void ConfigureServices(IServiceCollection services)
{
    services.AddControllersWithViews();
}
```

In both cases, the method gets `IServiceCollection`, which is already filled with a bunch of services that are required by ASP.NET Core. This service was added by the hosting services and parts of ASP.NET Core that are executed before the `ConfigureServices` method is called.

Inside the method, some more services are added. First, a configuration class that contains cookie policy options is added to `ServiceCollection`. In the following sample, you can also see a custom service called `MyService` that implements the `IService` interface. After that, the `AddMvc()` method adds another bunch of services required by the MVC framework. So far, we have around 140 services registered to `IServiceCollection`. However, the service collection isn't the actual DI container.

The actual DI container is wrapped in the so-called **service provider**, which will be created out of the service collection. `IServiceCollection` has an extension method registered to create `IServiceProvider` out of the service collection, which you can see in the following code snippet:

```
IServiceProvider provider = services.BuildServiceProvider()
```

`ServiceProvider` contains the immutable container that cannot be changed at runtime. With the default `ConfigureServices` method, the `IServiceProvider` is created in the background after this method was called.

Next, we'll learn more about applying an alternative `ServiceProvider` type as part of the DI customization process.

Using a different ServiceProvider type

Changing to a different or custom DI container is relatively easy if the other container already supports ASP.NET Core. Usually, the other container will use `IServiceCollection` to feed its own container. The third-party DI containers move the already registered services to the other container by looping over the collection:

1. Let's start by using `Autofac` as a third-party container. Type the following command into your command line to load the NuGet package:

    ```
    dotnet add package Autofac.Extensions.DependencyInjection
    ```

    `Autofac` is good for this because you are easily able to see what is happening here.

2. To register a custom IoC container, you need to register a different
    `IServiceProviderFactory` interface. In that case, you'll want to
    use `AutofacServiceProviderFactory` if you use `Autofac`.
    `IserviceProviderFactory` will create a `ServiceProvider` instance.
    The third-party container should provide one, if it supports ASP.NET Core.

    You should place this small extension method in `Program.cs` to register
    `AutofacServiceProviderFactory` with `IHostBuilder`:

    ```
    public static class IHostBuilderExtension
    {
        public static IHostBuilder
          UseAutofacServiceProviderFactory(
            this IHostBuilder hostbuilder)
        {
            hostbuilder.UseServiceProviderFactory
              <ContainerBuilder>(
            new AutofacServiceProviderFactory());
            return hostbuilder;
        }
    }
    ```

3. To use this extension method, you can change the `CreateHostBuilder`
    method slightly:

    ```
    public static IHostBuilder CreateHostBuilder(string[]
      args) =>
        Host.CreateDefaultBuilder(args)
            .UseAutofacServiceProviderFactory()
            .ConfigureWebHostDefaults(webBuilder =>
            {
                webBuilder.UseStartup<Startup>();
            });
    ```

This adds the `AutofacServiceProviderFactory` function to `IHostBuilder`
and enables the `Autofac` IoC container. If you have this in place, you will be able to use
`Autofac` as you like. In `Startup.cs`, you are able to use `IServiceCollection` to
register the dependencies or to add an additional method called `ConfigureContainer`
to do it the Autofac way.

Registering dependencies with ConfigureContainer

`ConfigureContainer` is where you can register things directly with `Autofac`. This runs after the `ConfigureServices` method, so the things here will override registrations made in `ConfigureServices`:

```
public void ConfigureContainer(ContainerBuilder builder)
{
    builder.RegisterType<MyService>().As<IService>();
    // custom service
}
```

The custom `MyService` service now gets registered using the Autofac way. In the next section, we'll introduce a useful package called Scrutor.

Introducing Scrutor

You don't always need to replace the existing .NET Core DI container to get and use some cool features. At the beginning of this chapter, I mentioned the autoregistration of services, which can be done with other DI containers. This can also be done with a nice NuGet package called **Scrutor** (`https://github.com/khellang/Scrutor`) by *Kristian Hellang* (`https://kristian.hellang.com`). Scrutor extends `IServiceCollection` to automatically register services with the .NET Core DI container.

> **Note**
>
> Andrew Lock has published a pretty detailed blog post relating to Scrutor. Rather than just repeating what he said, I suggest that you just go ahead and read that post to learn more about it: *Using Scrutor to automatically register your services with the ASP.NET Core DI container*, which is available at `https://andrewlock.net/using-scrutor-to-automatically-register-your-services-with-the-asp-net-core-di-container/`.

Summary

Using the approaches we have demonstrated in this chapter, you will be able to use any .NET Standard-compatible DI container to replace the existing one. If the container of your choice doesn't include a `ServiceProvider`, create your own that implements `IServiceProvider` and uses the DI container inside. If the container of your choice doesn't provide a method to populate the registered services in the container, create your own method. Loop over the registered services and add them to the other container.

Actually, the last step sounds easy, but can be a hard task, because you need to translate all the possible `IServiceCollection` registrations into registrations of the different container. The complexity of that task depends on the implementation details of the other DI container.

Anyway, you have the choice to use any DI container that is compatible with the .NET Standard. You can change a lot of the default implementations in ASP.NET Core.

This is also something you can do with the default HTTPS behavior on Windows, which we will learn more about in the next chapter.

4

Configuring and Customizing HTTPS with Kestrel

HTTPS is on by default and is a first-class feature. On Windows, the certificate that is needed to enable HTTPS is loaded from the Windows certificate store. If you create a project on Linux or Mac, the certificate is loaded from a certificate file.

Even if you want to create a project to run it behind an IIS or an NGINX web server, HTTPS is enabled. Usually, you would manage the certificate on the IIS or NGINX web server in that case. This shouldn't be a problem, however, so don't disable HTTPS in the ASP.NET Core settings.

Managing the certificate within the ASP.NET Core application directly makes sense if you run services behind the firewall, services that are not accessible from the internet; services such as background services for a microservice-based application, or services in a self-hosted ASP.NET Core application.

There are some scenarios where it makes sense to also load the certificate from a file on Windows as well. This could be in an application that you will run on Docker for Windows or Linux. Personally, I like the flexible way of loading the certificate from a file.

Only two topics will be covered in this short chapter:

- Introducing Kestrel
- Setting up Kestrel

The topics in this chapter refer to the Host layer of the ASP.NET Core architecture:

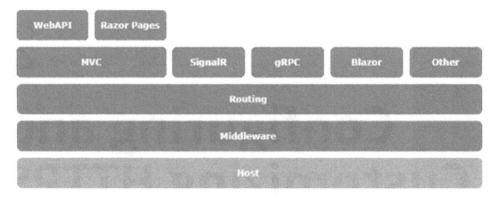

Figure 4.1 – ASP.NET Core architecture

Technical requirements

To follow the descriptions in this chapter, you will need to create an ASP.NET Core MVC application. Open your console, shell, or bash terminal, and change to your working directory. Use the following command to create a new MVC application:

```
dotnet new mvc -n HttpSample -o HttpSample
```

Now, open the project in Visual Studio by double-clicking the project file or, in VS Code, by typing the following command in the already open console:

```
cd HttpSample
code .
```

All of the code samples in this chapter can be found in the GitHub repository for this book at https://github.com/PacktPublishing/Customizing-ASP. NET-Core-5.0/tree/main/Chapter04.

Introducing Kestrel

Kestrel is a newly implemented HTTP server that is the hosting engine of ASP.NET Core. Every ASP.NET Core application will run on the Kestrel server. Classic ASP.NET applications (running on the .NET Framework) usually run directly on the IIS web server. With ASP.NET Core, Microsoft was inspired by **Node.js**, which also ships an HTTP server, called **Libuv**. In the first version of ASP.NET Core, Microsoft also used Libuv, and then added a layer on top called Kestrel. Node.js and ASP.NET Core shared the same HTTP server at that time.

Since the .NET Core framework has grown, and .NET Sockets was implemented on it, Microsoft has built its own HTTP server based on .NET Sockets, and removed Libuv, which was a dependency they don't own or control. Now, Kestrel is a full-featured HTTP server that runs ASP.NET Core applications.

The IIS web server acts as a reverse proxy that forwards the traffic to Kestrel and manages the Kestrel process. On Linux, usually NGINX is used as a reverse proxy for Kestrel.

Setting up Kestrel

As we did in the first two chapters of this book, we need to override the default `WebHostBuilder` type a little bit to set up Kestrel. With ASP.NET Core 3.0 and higher, it is possible to replace the default Kestrel base configuration with a custom configuration. This means that the Kestrel web server is configured to the host builder:

1. You will be able to add and configure Kestrel manually simply by using it. The following code shows what happens when you call the `UseKestrel()` method on `IwebHostBuilder`. Let's now see how this fits into the `CreateWebHostBuilder` method:

```
public class Program
{
    public static void Main(string[] args)
    {
        CreateWebHostBuilder(args).Build().Run();
    }

    public static IHostBuilder
        CreateHostBuilder(string[] args) =>
        Host.CreateDefaultBuilder(args)
            .ConfigureWebHostDefaults(webBuilder =>
```

```
{
    webBuilder
        .UseKestrel(options =>
        {
        })
        .UseStartup<Startup>();
}
}
```

The UseKestrel() method accepts an action to configure the Kestrel web server.

2. What we *actually* need to do is to configure the addresses and ports that the web server is listening on. For the HTTPS port, we also need to configure how the certificate should be loaded:

```
.UseKestrel(options =>
{
    options.Listen(IPAddress.Loopback, 5000);
    options.Listen(IPAddress.Loopback,  5001,
    listenOptions  =>
    {
        listenOptions.UseHttps("certificate.pfx",
            "topsecret");
    });
})
```

In this snippet, we add the addresses and ports to listen on. The second is defined as a secure endpoint configured to use HTTPS. The UseHttps() method is overloaded multiple times, to load certificates from the Windows Certificate Store as well as from files. In this case, we will use a file called certificate.pfx located in the project folder.

3. To create a certificate file to just play around with this configuration, open the certificate store and export the development certificate created by Visual Studio. It is located in the current user certificates under the personal certificates:

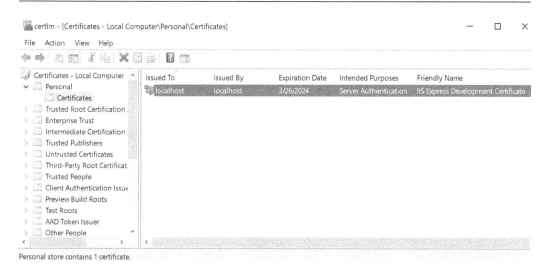

Figure 4.2 – Certificates

Right-click this entry. In the context menu, go to **All Tasks** and click **Export**. In the Certificate Export Wizard, choose **Yes, export the private key** and choose the .PFX format in the next screen. Click **Next**. Here, you need to set a password. This is the exact same password you will need to use in the code, as seen in the samples. Choose a filename and a location to store the file and press **Next**. The last screen will show a summary. Press **Finish** to save the certificate to a file.

For your safety

Use the following line *ONLY* to play around with this configuration:

```
listenOptions.UseHttps("certificate.pfx", "topsecret");
```

The problem is the hardcoded password. Never, *ever* store a password in a code file that gets pushed to any source code repository. Ensure that you load the password from the configuration API of ASP.NET Core. Use the user secrets on your local development machine and use environment variables on a server. On Azure, use the application settings to store the passwords. Passwords will be hidden on the Azure portal UI if they are marked as passwords.

Summary

This is just a small customization, but it should help if you want to share the code between different platforms, or if you want to run your application on Docker and don't want to worry about certificate stores, and so on.

Usually, if you run your application behind a web server such as IIS or NGINX, you don't need to care about certificates in your ASP.NET Core 5.0 application. However, if you host your application inside another application, on Docker or without an IIS or NGINX, you will need to.

ASP.NET Core 5.0 has a new feature to run tasks in the background inside the application. This topic will be covered in the next chapter.

5
Using IHostedService and BackgroundService

This fifth chapter isn't really about customization; it's more about a feature you can use to create background services to run tasks asynchronously inside your application. I use this feature to regularly fetch data from a remote service in a small ASP.NET Core application.

We'll examine the following topics:

- Introducing `IHostedService`
- Introducing `BackgroundService`
- Implementing the new Worker Service projects

The topics of this chapter refer to the Host layer of the ASP.NET Core architecture:

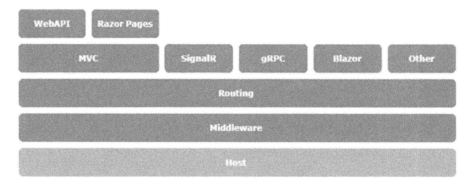

Figure 5.1 – ASP.NET Core architecture

Technical requirements

To follow the descriptions in this chapter, you will need to create an ASP.NET Core application. Open your console, shell, or bash terminal, and change to your working directory. Use the following command to create a new MVC application:

```
dotnet new mvc -n HostedServiceSample -o HostedServiceSample
```

Now open the project in Visual Studio by double-clicking the project file or in VS Code by changing the folder to the project and typing the following command in the already open console:

```
cd HostedServiceSample
code .
```

All of the code samples of this chapter can be found in the GitHub repo for this book: https://github.com/PacktPublishing/Customizing-ASP.NET-Core-5.0/tree/main/Chapter05.

Introducing IHostedService

Hosted services have been a thing since ASP.NET Core 2.0 and can be used to run tasks asynchronously in the background of your application. They can be used to fetch data periodically, do some calculations in the background, or to do some cleanups. You can also use them to send preconfigured emails – or whatever you need to do in the background.

Hosted services are basically simple classes that implement the `IHostedService` interface. You call them with the following code:

```
public class SampleHostedService : IHostedService
{
    public Task StartAsync(CancellationToken
      cancellationToken)
    {
    }

    public Task StopAsync(CancellationToken
      cancellationToken)
    {
    }
}
```

`IHostedService` needs to implement a `StartAsync()` method and a `StopAsync()` method. The `StartAsync()` method is the place where you implement the logic to execute. This method gets executed once, immediately after the application starts. The `StopAsync()` method, on the other hand, gets executed just before the application stops. This also means that to start a scheduled service, you will need to implement it on your own. You will need to implement a loop that executes the code regularly.

To execute `IHostedService`, you will need to register it in the ASP.NET Core dependency injection container as a singleton instance:

```
services.AddSingleton<IHostedService,
    SampleHostedService>();
```

The next sample shows you how hosted services work. It writes a log message on start, on stop, and every 2 seconds, to the console:

1. First, write the class skeleton that retrieves `ILogger` via `DependencyInjection`:

    ```
    public class SampleHostedService : IHostedService
    {
        private readonly ILogger<SampleHostedService>
            logger;
    ```

```
    // inject a logger
    public
        SampleHostedService(ILogger<SampleHostedService>
          logger)
    {
        this.logger = logger;
    }

    public Task StartAsync(CancellationToken
      cancellationToken)
    {
    }

    public Task StopAsync(CancellationToken
      cancellationToken)
    {
    }
}
```

2. The next step is to implement the `StopAsync` method. This method is used to clean up in case you need to close connections, streams, and so on:

```
public Task StopAsync(CancellationToken
  cancellationToken)
{
    logger.LogInformation("Hosted service stopping");
    return Task.CompletedTask;
}
```

3. The actual work will be done in `StartAsync`:

```
public Task StartAsync(CancellationToken
  cancellationToken)
{
    logger.LogInformation("Hosted service starting");

    return Task.Factory.StartNew(async () =>
    {
        // loop until a cancelation is requested
        while
        (!cancellationToken.IsCancellationRequested)
        {
            logger.LogInformation($"Hosted service
              executing - {DateTime.Now}");
            try
            {
                // wait for 2 seconds
                await
                  Task.Delay(TimeSpan.FromSeconds(2),
                  cancellationToken);
            }
            catch (OperationCanceledException) { }
        }
    }, cancellationToken);
}
```

4. To test this, start the application by calling the next command in the console:

```
dotnet run
```

Or press *F5* in Visual Studio or VS Code. This results in the following console output:

```
λ dotnet run
Using launch settings from C:\git\dotnetconf\005-hostedservices\HostedServiceSamp
le\Properties\launchSettings.json...
info: Microsoft.AspNetCore.DataProtection.KeyManagement.XmlKeyManager[0]
      User profile is available. Using 'C:\Users\Juergen\AppData\Local\ASP.NET\Da
taProtection-Keys' as key repository and Windows DPAPI to encrypt keys at rest.
info: HostedServiceSample.SampleHostedService[0]
      Hosted service starting
info: HostedServiceSample.SampleHostedService[0]
      Hosted service executing - 10/01/2018 06:55:49
Hosting environment: Development
Content root path: C:\git\dotnetconf\005-hostedservices\HostedServiceSample
Now listening on: https://localhost:5001
Now listening on: http://localhost:5000
Application started. Press Ctrl+C to shut down.
info: HostedServiceSample.SampleHostedService[0]
      Hosted service executing - 10/01/2018 06:55:51
info: HostedServiceSample.SampleHostedService[0]
      Hosted service executing - 10/01/2018 06:55:53
info: HostedServiceSample.SampleHostedService[0]
      Hosted service executing - 10/01/2018 06:55:55
info: HostedServiceSample.SampleHostedService[0]
      Hosted service executing - 10/01/2018 06:55:57
Application is shutting down...
^C
infoC:\git\dotnetconf\005-hostedservices\HostedServiceSample
: HostedServiceSample.SampleHostedService[0]
      Hosted service stopping
λ
```

Figure 5.2 – A screenshot of the dotnet run output

As you can see, the log output is written to the console every 2 seconds.

In the next section, we will look at `BackgroundService`.

Introducing BackgroundService

The `BackgroundService` class is new in ASP.NET Core 3.0 and is basically an abstract class that already implements the `IHostedService` interface. It also provides an abstract method, `ExecuteAsync()`, which returns a `Task` type.

If you want to reuse the hosted service from the last section, the code will need to be rewritten. Follow the next steps to learn how:

1. First, write the class skeleton that retrieves `ILogger` via `DependencyInjection`:

    ```
    public class SampleBackgroundService :
        BackgroundService
    {
    ```

```
        private readonly ILogger<SampleHostedService>
          logger;

        // inject a logger
        public SampleBackgroundService(
            ILogger<SampleHostedService> logger)
        {
            this.logger = logger;
        }
    }
```

You might wish to add the following `using` statements at the beginning of the file:

```
using Microsoft.Extensions.Hosting;
using Microsoft.Extensions.Logging;
using System.Threading;
```

2. The next step would be to override the `StopAsync` method:

```
public override async Task StopAsync(CancellationToken
  cancellationToken)
{
    logger.LogInformation("Background service
      stopping");
    await Task.CompletedTask;
}
```

3. In the last step, we will override the `ExecuteAsync` method that does all the work:

```
protected override async Task
  ExecuteAsync(CancellationToken cancellationToken)
{
    logger.LogInformation("Background service
      starting");

    await Task.Factory.StartNew(async () =>
    {
        while
          (!cancellationToken.IsCancellationRequested)
        {
```

```
            logger.LogInformation($"Background service
              executing - {DateTime.Now}");
         try
         {
             await
               Task.Delay(TimeSpan.FromSeconds(2),
                  cancellationToken);
         }
         catch (OperationCanceledException) {}
       }
    }, cancellationToken);
  }
```

Even the registration is new.

Additionally, in ASP.NET Core 3.0, `ServiceCollection` has a new extension method to register hosted services or a background worker:

```
services.AddHostedService<SampleBackgroundService>();
```

Next, let's take a look at Worker Service projects.

Implementing the new Worker Service projects

The new **Worker Services** and the generic hosting in ASP.NET Core 3.0 and later make it pretty easy to create simple service-like applications that can do some stuff without the full blown ASP.NET stack – and without a web server.

You can create this project with the following command:

```
dotnet new worker -n BackgroundServiceSample -o
BackgroundServiceSample
```

Basically, this creates a console application with `Program.cs` and `Worker.cs` in it. The `Worker.cs` file contains the `BackgroundService` class. The `Program.cs` file looks pretty familiar but without `WebHostBuilder`:

```
public class Program
{
    public static void Main(string[] args)
```

```
    {
        CreateHostBuilder(args).Build().Run();
    }

    public static IHostBuilder CreateHostBuilder(string[]
      args) =>
        Host.CreateDefaultBuilder(args)
            .ConfigureServices((hostContext, services) =>
            {
                services.AddHostedService<Worker>();
            });
}
```

This creates an `IHostBuilder` type with dependency injection enabled. This means we are able to use dependency injection in any kind of application, not only in ASP.NET Core applications.

Then the worker is added to the service collection.

Where is this useful? You can run this app as a Windows service or as a background application in a Docker container, which doesn't need an HTTP endpoint.

Summary

You can now start to do some more complex things with `IHostedService` and the `BackgroundService`. Be careful with background services, because they all run in the same application; if you use too much CPU or memory, this could slow down your application.

For bigger applications, I would suggest running such tasks in a separate application that is specialized for executing background tasks: a separate Docker container, a `BackgroundWorker` type on Azure, Azure Functions, or something like that. However, it should be separate from the main application in that case.

In the next chapter, we will learn about middleware, and how you can use them to implement special logic on the request pipeline, or serve specific logic on different paths.

6
Writing Custom Middleware

Wow, we are already onto the sixth chapter of this book! In this chapter, we will learn about **middleware** and how you can use it to customize your app a little more. We will quickly go through the basics of middleware and then we'll explore some special things you can do with middleware.

We'll cover the following topics:

- Introducing middleware
- Writing a custom middleware
- Exploring the potential of middleware
- Using middleware on ASP.NET Core 3.0 and later

The topics of this chapter relate to the **Middleware** layer of the ASP.NET Core architecture:

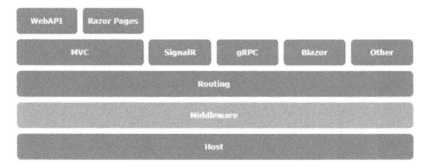

Figure 6.1 – ASP.NET Core architecture

Technical requirements

To follow the descriptions in this chapter, you will need to create an ASP.NET Core MVC application. Open your console, shell, or bash terminal, and change to your working directory. Use the following command to create a new MVC application:

```
dotnet new web -n MiddlewaresSample -o MiddlewaresSample
```

Now, open the project in Visual Studio by double-clicking the project file, or in VS Code by typing the following command in the already open console:

```
cd MiddlewaresSample
code .
```

All of the code samples of this chapter can be found in the GitHub repo for this book: https://github.com/PacktPublishing/Customizing-ASP.NET-Core-5.0/tree/main/Chapter06.

Introducing middleware

The majority of readers probably already know what middleware is, but some of you might not. Even if you have already been using ASP.NET Core for a while, you don't really need to know details about middleware, because they are mostly hidden behind nicely named extension methods such as UseMvc(), UseAuthentication(), UseDeveloperExceptionPage(), and so on. Every time you call a Use method in the Startup.cs file, in the Configure method, you'll implicitly use at least one, maybe more, middleware.

A **middleware** is a piece of code that handles the request pipeline. Imagine the request pipeline as a huge tube you can call something in to and an echo comes back. The middleware is responsible for the creation of this echo, manipulating the sound to enrich the information, handling the source sound, or handling the echo.

Middleware is executed in the order in which it is configured. The first middleware configured is the first that gets executed.

In an ASP.NET Core web, if the client requests an image or any other static file, the StaticFileMiddleware type searches for that resource and returns that resource if it finds it. If not, this middleware does nothing except call the next one. If there is no final middleware that handles the request pipeline, the request returns nothing. The MvcMiddleware type also checks the requested resource, tries to map it to a configured route, executes the controller, creates a view, and returns an HTML or Web API result. If the MvcMiddleware type does not find a matching controller, it will return a result anyway; in this case, it is a *404 Status* result. It returns an echo in any case. This is why the MvcMiddleware type is the last middleware configured:

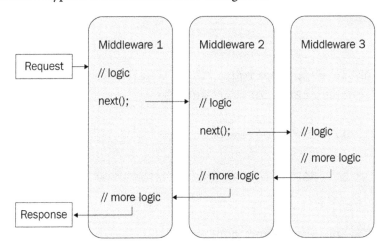

Figure 6.2 – Middleware workflow diagram

An **exception handling** middleware is usually one of the first middleware configured, not because it is the first to be executed but because it is the last. The first middleware configured is also the last one to be executed if the echo comes back from the tube. An exception handling middleware validates the result and displays a possible exception in the browser and client in a friendly way. This is where a runtime error gets a *500 Status*:

1. You are able to see how the pipeline is executed if you create an empty ASP.NET Core application as described in the *Technical requirements* section.

2. Open Startup.cs with your favorite editor. It should be pretty empty compared to a regular ASP.NET Core application. Rewrite the Configure() method like this:

```
public class Startup
{
    public void ConfigureServices(IServiceCollection
        services)
    {
    }

    public void Configure(IApplicationBuilder app,
        IWebHostEnvironment env)
    {
        if (env.IsDevelopment())
        {
            app.UseDeveloperExceptionPage();
        }

        app.Run(async context =>
        {
            await context.Response.WriteAsync("Hello
                World!");
        });
    }
}
```

Here, the `DeveloperExceptionPageMiddleware` type is used, with a special lambda middleware that only writes `"Hello World!"` to the response stream. The response stream is the echo we learned about previously. This special middleware stops the pipeline and returns something like an echo. So, it is the last middleware to run.

3. Leave this middleware and add the following lines right before the `app.Run()` function:

```
app.Use(async (context, next) =>{
    await context.Response.WriteAsync("===");
    await next();
    await context.Response.WriteAsync("===");
});

app.Use(async (context, next) =>
{
    await context.Response.WriteAsync(">>>>>> ");
    await next();
    await context.Response.WriteAsync(" <<<<<<");
});
```

These two calls of `app.Use()` also create two lambda middleware, but this time, in addition to dealing with specific requests, the middleware are calling their successors: each middleware knows which middleware should follow it, and calls it. Both middleware write to the response stream before and after the next middleware is called. Before the next middleware is called, the actual request is handled, and after the next middleware is called, the response (echo) is handled. This should demonstrate how the pipeline works.

4. If you now run the application (using `dotnet run`) and open the displayed URL in the browser, you should see a plaintext result like this:

```
===>>>>>> Hello World! <<<<<<===
```

Does this make sense to you? If yes, let's move on and see how to use this concept to add some additional functionality to the request pipeline.

Writing a custom middleware

ASP.NET Core is based on middleware. All the logic that gets executed during a request is based on middleware. So, we can use this to add custom functionality to the web. We want to know the execution time of every request that goes through the request pipeline:

1. We can do this by creating and starting a stopwatch before the next middleware is called, and by stopping measuring the execution time after the next middleware is called, like so:

```
app.Use(async (context, next) =>
{
    var s = new Stopwatch();
    s.Start();

    // execute the rest of the pipeline
    await next();

    s.Stop(); //stop measuring
    var result = s.ElapsedMilliseconds;

    // write out the milliseconds needed
    await context.Response.WriteAsync($"Time needed:
       {result}");
});
```

After that, we return the elapsed milliseconds to the response stream.

2. If you write some more middleware, the `Configure` method in `Startup.cs` gets pretty messy. This is why most middleware is written as separate classes. This could look like this:

```
public class StopwatchMiddleWare
{
    private readonly RequestDelegate _next;

    public StopwatchMiddleWare(RequestDelegate next)
    {
        _next = next;
    }
```

```
public async Task Invoke(HttpContext context)
{
    var s = new Stopwatch();
    s.Start();

    // execute the rest of the pipeline
    await _next(context);

    s.Stop(); //stop measuring
    var result = s.ElapsedMilliseconds;

    // write out the milliseconds needed
    await context.Response.WriteAsync($"Time
      needed: {result}");
}
}
```

This way, we get the next middleware via the constructor and the current context in the Invoke() method.

> **Note**
> The middleware is initialized at the start of the application and the constructor runs only once during the application lifetime. On the other hand, the Invoke() method is called once per request.

3. To use this middleware, there is a generic UseMiddleware() method available you can use in the configure method:

```
app.UseMiddleware<StopwatchMiddleware>();
```

4. The more elegant way is to create an extension method that encapsulates this call:

```
public static class StopwatchMiddlewareExtension
{
    public static IApplicationBuilder
      UseStopwatch(this IApplicationBuilder app)
    {
        app.UseMiddleware<StopwatchMiddleware>();
```

```
            return app;
        }
    }
```

5. Now you can simply call it like this:

```
app.UseStopwatch();
```

This is the way you can provide additional functionality to an ASP.NET Core application through the request pipeline. You have the entire `HttpContext` available in your middleware. With this, you can manipulate the request or even the response using middleware.

The `AuthenticationMiddleware` type, for example, tries to collect user information from the request. If it doesn't find any, it will ask for the information by sending a specific response back to the client. If it finds some information, it will add it to the request context and make it available to the entire application this way.

Exploring the potential of middleware

There are many other things you can do with middleware. For example, did you know that you can split the request pipeline into two or more pipelines? We'll look at how to do that and several other things in this section.

Branching the pipeline with /map

The next snippet shows how to create branches based on specific paths:

```
app.Map("/map1", app1 =>
{
    // some more Middleware

    app1.Run(async context =>
    {
        await context.Response.WriteAsync("Map Test 1");
    });
});

app.Map("/map2", app2 =>
{
```

```
    // some more Middleware

    app2.Run(async context =>
    {
        await context.Response.WriteAsync("Map Test 2");
    });
});

    // some more Middleware

app.Run(async (context) =>
{
    await context.Response.WriteAsync("Hello World!");
});
```

The path "/map1" is a specific branch that continues the request pipeline inside – the same with "/map2". Both maps have their own middleware configurations inside. All other unspecified paths will follow the main branch.

Branching the pipeline with MapWhen()

There is also a MapWhen() method to branch the pipeline based on a condition instead of a branch based on a path:

```
public void Configure(IApplicationBuilder app)
{
    app.MapWhen(
        context =>
           context.Request.Query.ContainsKey("branch"),
        app1 =>
        {
            // some more Middleware

            app1.Run(async context =>
            {
                await context.Response.WriteAsync(
                    "MapBranch Test");
            });
```

```
    });

    // some more Middleware

    app.Run(async context =>
    {
        await context.Response.WriteAsync(
            "Hello from non-Map delegate.");
    });
}
```

Next, we'll look at using middleware to create conditions.

Creating conditions with middleware

You can create conditions based on configuration values or, as shown here, based on properties of the request context. In the previous example, a query string property is used. You can use HTTP headers, form properties, or any other property of the request context.

You are also able to nest the maps to create child and grandchild branches if needed.

Map() or MapWhen() can be used to provide a special API or resource based on a specific path or a specific condition. The ASP.NET Core HealthCheck API is done like this: first, it uses MapWhen() to specify the port to use, and then Map() to set the path for the HealthCheck API (or it uses Map() if no port is specified). In the end, the HealthCheckMiddleware type is used. The following code is just an example to show what it looks like:

```
private static void UseHealthChecksCore(IApplicationBuilder
    app, PathString path, int? port, object[] args)
{
    if (port == null)
    {
        app.Map(path,
            b =>
                b.UseMiddleware<HealthCheckMiddleware>(args));
    }
    else
    {
        app.MapWhen(
```

```
                    c => c.Connection.LocalPort == port,
                    b0 => b0.Map(path,
                    b1 =>
                        b1.UseMiddleware<HealthCheckMiddleware> (args)
                    )
            );
        }
}
```

Next, let's see how you should use terminating middleware in newer versions of
ASP.NET Core.

Using middleware on ASP.NET Core 3.0 and later

In ASP.NET Core 3.0 and later, the Configure() method looks different. There are two
new kinds of middleware elements, called UseRouting and UseEndpoints:

```
public void Configure(IApplicationBuilder app,
    IWebHostEnvironment env)
{
    if (env.IsDevelopment())
    {
        app.UseDeveloperExceptionPage();
    }

    app.UseRouting();

    app.UseEndpoints(endpoints =>
    {
        endpoints.MapGet("/", async context =>
        {
            await context.Response.WriteAsync("Hell World!");
        });
    });
}
```

The first one is a middleware that uses routing and the other one uses endpoints. What exactly are we looking at?

This is the new **endpoint routing**. Previously, routing was part of MVC and only worked with MVC, Web APIs, and frameworks that are based on the MVC framework. In ASP. NET Core 3.0 and later, however, routing is no longer in the MVC framework. Now, MVC and the other frameworks are mapped to a specific route or endpoint. There are different kinds of endpoint definitions available.

In the preceding snippet, a GET request is mapped to the page root URL. In the next snippet, MVC is mapped to a route pattern and **Razor Pages** are mapped to the *razor pages* specific file structure based routes:

```
app.UseEndpoints(endpoints =>
{
    endpoints.MapControllerRoute(
        name: "default",
        pattern: "{controller=Home}/{action=Index}/{id?}");
    endpoints.MapRazorPages();
});
```

There is no UseMvc() anymore, even if it still exists and still works on the IApplicationBiulder level to prevent existing code from breaking. Now, there are new methods to activate ASP.NET Core features more granularly.

These are the most commonly used new Map methods for ASP.NET Core 5.0:

- **Areas for MVC and WebAPI**: endpoints.
  MapAreaControllerRoute(...);
- **MVC and WebAPI**: endpoints.MapControllerRoute(...);
- **Blazor Server Side**: endpoints.MapBlazorHub(...);
- **SignalR**: endpoints.MapHub(...);
- **Razor Pages**: endpoints.MapRazorPages(...);
- **Health Checks**: endpoints.MapHealthChecks(...);

There are a lot more methods to define fallback endpoints and to map routes and HTTP methods to delegates and middleware.

If you want to create middleware that works on all requests, such as the `StopWatchMiddleware` type, this will work as before on the `IApplicationBuilder` type. If you would like to write a middleware to work on a specific path or route, you will need to create a `Map` method for it to map to that route.

> **Important note**
>
> It is no longer recommended to handle the route inside the middleware. With this approach, the middleware is a lot more generic and will work on multiple routes with a single configuration.

I recently wrote a middleware to provide a GraphQL endpoint in an ASP.NET Core application; I had to rewrite it to follow the new ASP.NET Core routing. The old way would still have worked but would have handled the paths and routes separately from the new ASP.NET Core routing. Let's look at how to deal with those situations.

Rewriting a terminating middleware to current standards

If you have an existing middleware that provides a different endpoint, you should change it to use the new endpoint routing:

1. As an example, let's create a small dummy middleware that writes an application status to a specific route. In this demo, there is no custom route handling:

```
public class AppStatusMiddleware
{
    private readonly RequestDelegate _next;
    private readonly string _status;


    public AppStatusMiddleware(
        RequestDelegate next, string status)
    {
        _next = next;
        _status = status;
    }

    public async Task Invoke(HttpContext context)
    {
```

```
        await context.Response.WriteAsync(
            $"Hello {_status}!");
    }
}
```

The first thing we need to do is to write an extension method on the IEndpointRouteBuilder type. This method has a route pattern as an optional argument and returns an IEndpointConventionBuilder type to enable CORS, authentication, or other conditions to the route.

2. Now we should add an extension method to make it easier to use the middleware:

```
public static class MapAppStatusMiddlewareExtension
{
    public static IEndpointConventionBuilder
      MapAppStatus(
        this IEndpointRouteBuilder routes,
        string pattern = "/",
        string name = "World")
    {
        var pipeline = routes
            .CreateApplicationBuilder()
            .UseMiddleware<AppStatusMiddleware>(name)
            .Build();

        return routes.Map(pattern, pipeline)
            .WithDisplayName("AppStatusMiddleware");
    }
}
```

3. Once that is complete, we can use the MapAppStatus method to map it to a specific route:

```
app.UseEndpoints(endpoints =>
{
    endpoints.MapGet("/", async context =>
    {
        await context.Response.WriteAsync(
            "Hello World!");
```

```
        });


        endpoints.MapAppStatus("/status", "Status");
    });
```

4. We can now call the route in the browser: `http://localhost:5000/status`.

We will learn more about endpoint routing and how to customize it in *Chapter 13, Working with Endpoint Routing*. For now, let's recap what we've learned about middleware.

Summary

Most of the ASP.NET Core features are based on middleware and we are able to extend ASP.NET Core by creating our own middleware.

In the next two chapters, we will have a look at different data types and how to handle them using content negotiation. We will learn how to create API outputs with any format and data type.

7

Content Negotiation Using a Custom OutputFormatter

In this seventh chapter, we are going to learn about how to send your data to the client in different formats and types. By default, the ASP.NET Core Web API sends data as JSON, but there are some more ways to distribute data.

We'll cover the following sections:

- Introducing `OutputFomatters`
- Creating custom `OutputFormatters`

The topics of this chapter relate to the **WebAPI** layer of the ASP.NET Core architecture:

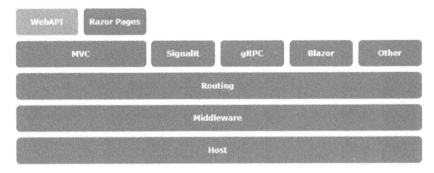

Figure 7.1 – ASP.NET Core architecture

Technical requirements

To follow the descriptions in this chapter, you will need to create an ASP.NET Core MVC application. Open your console, shell, or bash terminal, and change to your working directory. Use the following command to create a new MVC application:

```
dotnet new webapi -n OutputFormatterSample -o
OutputFormatterSample
```

Now, open the project in Visual Studio by double-clicking the project file, or in VS Code by typing the following command in the already open console:

```
cd OutputFormatterSample
code .
```

All of the code samples of this chapter can be found in the GitHub repo for this book: https://github.com/PacktPublishing/Customizing-ASP. NET-Core-5.0/tree/main/Chapter07.

Introducing OutputFormatters

OutputFormatters are classes that transform your existing data into different formats to send it through HTTP to clients. The Web API uses a default `OutputFormatters` to turn objects into JSON, which is the default format to send structured data. Other built-in formatters include an XML formatter and a plain text formatter.

With so-called *content negotiation*, clients are able to decide which format they want to retrieve. The client needs to specify the content type of the format in the `Accept` header. Content negotiation is implemented in `ObjectResult`.

By default, the Web API always returns JSON, even if you accept text/XML in the header. This is why the built-in XML formatter is not registered by default.

There are two ways to add `XmlSerializerOutputFormatter` to ASP.NET Core. The first is shown in the following code snippet:

```
services.AddControllers()
    .AddXmlSerializerFormatters();
```

Or, alternatively, you can use the following:

```
services.AddControllers()
    .AddMvcOptions(options =>
    {
        options.OutputFormatters.Add(
            new XmlSerializerOutputFormatter());
    });
```

You might need to add the `Microsoft.AspNetCore.Mvc.Formatters` namespace to the `using` statements.

There is also `XmlDataContractSerializerOutputFormatter` available that uses `DataContractSerializer` internally, which is more flexible in configuration.

By default, any `Accept` header will automatically be turned into `application/json` even if you use one of these methods. However, we can fix that.

If you want to allow the clients to accept different headers, you need to switch that translation off:

```
services.AddControllers()
    .AddMvcOptions(options =>
    {
        options.RespectBrowserAcceptHeader = true;
            // false by default
    });
```

Some third-party components that don't completely support ASP.NET Core 5.0 won't write asynchronously to the response stream but the default configuration, since ASP.NET Core 3.0 *only* allows asynchronous writing.

To enable synchronous writing access, you will need to add these lines to the `ConfigureServices` method:

```
services.Configure<KestrelServerOptions>(options =>
{
    options.AllowSynchronousIO = true;
});
```

Add the `Microsoft.AspNetCore.Server.Kestrel.Core` namespace to the `using` statements to get access to the options.

To try the formatters, let's set up a small test project.

Preparing a test project

Using the console, we will create a small ASP.NET Core Web API project:

1. Execute the following commands to add the necessary NuGet packages:

    ```
    dotnet add package GenFu
    dotnet add package CsvHelper
    ```

    This creates a new Web API project and adds two NuGet packages to it. `GenFu` is an awesome library to easily create test data. The second package, `CsvHelper`, helps us to easily write CSV data.

    Now, open the project in Visual Studio or in VS Code and create a new controller called `PersonsController` in the `controller` folder:

    ```
    [Route("api/[controller]")]
    [ApiController]
    public class PersonsController : ControllerBase
    {
    }
    ```

2. Open `PersonsController.cs` and add a `Get()` method like this:

```
[HttpGet]
public ActionResult<IEnumerable<Person>> Get()
{
    var persons = A.ListOf<Person>(25);
    return persons;
}
```

You might need to add the following `using` statements at the beginning of the file:

```
using GenFu;
using OutputFormatterSample.models;
```

This creates a list of 25 persons by using `GenFu`. The properties will automatically be filled with realistic data. **GenFu** is an open source, fast, lightweight, and extendable test data generator. It contains built-in lists of names, cities, countries, phone numbers, and so on, and fills the data automatically into the right properties of a class, depending on the property names. A property called `City` will be filled with the name of a city, and a property called `Phone`, `Telephone`, or `Phonenumber` will be filled with a well-formatted fake phone number. You'll see the magic of GenFu and the results later on.

3. Create a `models` folder and create a new file, `Person.cs`, with the `Person` class inside:

```
public class Person
{
    public int Id { get; set; }
    public string FirstName { get; set; }
    public string LastName { get; set; }
    public int Age { get; set; }
    public string EmailAddress { get; set; }
    public string Address { get; set; }
    public string City { get; set; }
    public string Phone { get; set; }
}
```

4. Open `Startup.cs` as well, add the XML formatters, and allow other **Accept** headers, as described earlier:

```
services.AddControllers()
    .AddMvcOptions(options =>
    {
        options.RespectBrowserAcceptHeader = true;
        // false by default
        options.OutputFormatters.Add(
            new XmlSerializerOutputFormatter());
    });
```

That's it for now. Now you are able to retrieve the data from the Web API.

5. Start the project by using the `dotnet run` command.

    Next, we'll test the API.

Testing the Web API

The best tools to test a Web API are **Fiddler** (`https://www.telerik.com/fiddler`) or Postman (`https://www.postman.com/`). I prefer Postman because I find it easier to use. In the end, it doesn't matter which tool you want to use; in these demos, we will use Postman:

1. In Postman, create a new request. Write the API URL, which is `https://localhost:5001/api/persons`, into the `address` field, and add a header with the key as `Accept` and the value as `application/json`.

    After clicking **Send**, you will see the JSON result in the response body, as shown in the following screenshot:

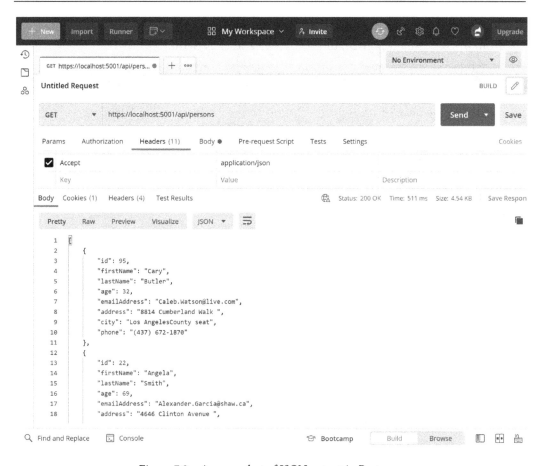

Figure 7.2 – A screenshot of JSON output in Postman

Here, you can see the autogenerated values. GenFu puts the data into the person's properties, based on the property type and the property name: real first names and real last names, as well as real cities and properly formatted phone numbers.

2. Next, let's test the XML output formatter. In Postman, change the `Accept` header from `application/json` to `text/xml` and click **Send**:

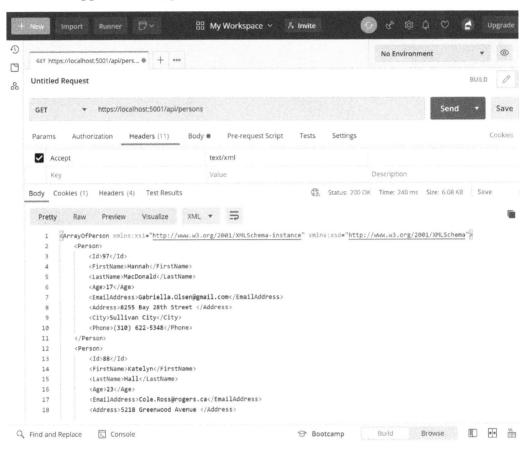

Figure 7.3 – A screenshot of XML output in Postman

We now have an XML formatted output.

Now, let's go a step further and create some custom `OutputFormatters`.

Creating custom OutputFormatters

The plan is to create a **VCard** output to be able to import the person's contact details directly to Outlook or any other contact database that supports VCards. Later in this section, we also want to create a CSV output formatter.

Both are text-based output formatters and will derive their values from
`TextOutputFormatter`:

1. Create a new class in a new file called `VcardOutputFormatter.cs`.

2. Now, insert the following class skeleton in the new file. You will find the
   implementations of the empty methods in the following snippets. The constructor
   contains the supported media types and content encodings:

```csharp
public class VcardOutputFormatter : TextOutputFormatter
{
    public string ContentType { get; }

    public VcardOutputFormatter()
    {
        SupportedMediaTypes.Add(
            MediaTypeHeaderValue.Parse("text/vcard"));

        SupportedEncodings.Add(Encoding.UTF8);
        SupportedEncodings.Add(Encoding.Unicode);
    }

    protected override bool CanWriteType(Type type)
    {
    }

    public override Task WriteResponseBodyAsync(
        OutputFormatterWriteContext context,
        Encoding selectedEncoding)
    {
    }

    private static void FormatVcard(
        StringBuilder buffer,
        Person person,
        ILogger logger)
```

```
        {
        }
    }
```

You might need to add the following using statements:

```
using Microsoft.AspNetCore.Mvc.Formatters;
using System.Text;
using Microsoft.Extensions.Logging;
using Microsoft.Net.Http.Headers;
```

3. The next snippet shows the implementation of the `CanWriteType` method. It is optional to override this method, but it makes sense to restrict it to a specific condition. In this case, the `OutputFormatter` can only format objects of type `Person`:

```
protected override bool CanWriteType(Type type)
{
    if (typeof(Person).IsAssignableFrom(type)
        || typeof(IEnumerable<Person>)
            .IsAssignableFrom(type))
    {
        return base.CanWriteType(type);
    }
    return false;
}
```

4. You need to override `WriteResponseBodyAsync` to convert the actual `Person` objects into the output you want to have. To get the objects to convert, you need to extract them from `OutputFormatterWriteContext` that gets passed into the method. You also get the HTTP response from this context. This is needed to write the results and send them to the client.

Inside the method, we check whether we get one person or a list of persons and call the not-yet-implemented `FormatVcard` method:

```
public override Task WriteResponseBodyAsync(
    OutputFormatterWriteContext context,
    Encoding selectedEncoding)
{
    var serviceProvider =
```

```
        context.HttpContext.RequestServices;
    var logger = serviceProvider.GetService(
        typeof(ILogger<VcardOutputFormatter>)) as
          ILogger;

    var response = context.HttpContext.Response;

    var buffer = new StringBuilder();
    if (context.Object is IEnumerable<Person>)
    {
        foreach (var person in context.Object as
          IEnumerable<Person>)
        {
            FormatVcard(buffer, person, logger);
        }
    }
    else
    {
        var person = context.Object as Person;
        FormatVcard(buffer, person, logger);
    }
    return response.WriteAsync(buffer.ToString());
}
```

5. To format the output to support standard `VCard`, you need to do some manual work:

```
private static void FormatVcard(
    StringBuilder buffer,
    Person person,
    ILogger logger)
{
    buffer.AppendLine("BEGIN:VCARD");
    buffer.AppendLine("VERSION:2.1");
    buffer.AppendLine(
        $"FN:{person.FirstName} {person.LastName}");
            buffer.AppendLine(
```

```
            $"N:{person.LastName};{person.FirstName}");
        buffer.AppendLine(
            $"EMAIL:{person.EmailAddress}");
        buffer.AppendLine(
            $"TEL;TYPE=VOICE,HOME:{person.Phone}");
        buffer.AppendLine(
            $"ADR;TYPE=home:;;{person.Address};{person.
                City}");
        buffer.AppendLine($"UID:{person.Id}");
        buffer.AppendLine("END:VCARD");


        logger.LogInformation(
            $"Writing {person.FirstName}
                {person.LastName}");
    }
```

6. Then, we need to register the new `VcardOutputFormatter` type in `Startup.cs`:

```
services.AddControllers()
    .AddMvcOptions(options =>
    {
        options.RespectBrowserAcceptHeader = true;
            // false by default
        options.OutputFormatters.Add(
            new XmlSerializerOutputFormatter());


        // register the VcardOutputFormatter
        options.OutputFormatters.Add(
            new VcardOutputFormatter());
    });
```

7. Start the app again using `dotnet run`.

8.   Now, change the `Accept` header to `text/vcard` and let's see what happens:

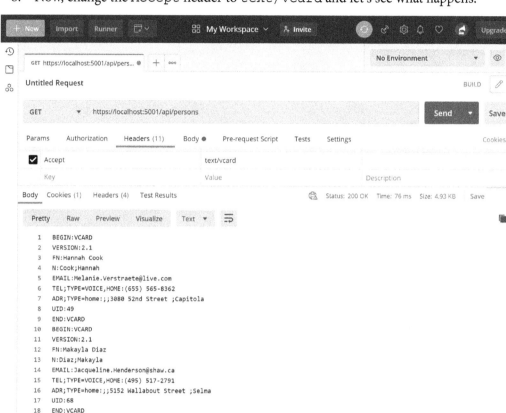

Figure 7.4 – A screenshot of VCard output in Postman

We now should see all of our data in the `VCard` format.

9.   Let's do the same for a CSV output. We already added the `CsvHelper` library to the project. Now go to the following URL and download `CsvOutputFormatter` to put it into your project: `https://github.com/PacktPublishing/ Customizing-ASP.NET-Core-5.0/blob/main/Chapter07/ OutputFormatterSample5.0/CsvOutputFormatter.cs`.

10. Let's have quick have a look at the `WriteResponseBodyAsync` method:

```
public override async Task WriteResponseBodyAsync(
    OutputFormatterWriteContext context,
    Encoding selectedEncoding)
{
    var response = context.HttpContext.Response;

    var csv = new CsvWriter(
        new StreamWriter(response.Body),
        CultureInfo.InvariantCulture);

    IEnumerable<Person> persons;
    if (context.Object is IEnumerable<Person>)
    {
        persons = context.Object as
            IEnumerable<Person>;
    }
    else
    {
        var person = context.Object as Person;
        persons = new List<Person> { person };
    }
    await csv.WriteRecordsAsync(persons);
}
```

11. This almost works the same way as `VcardOutputFormatter`. We can pass the response stream via `StreamWriter` directly into `CsvWriter`. After that, we are able to feed the persons or the list of persons to the writer. That's it.

12. We also need to register `CsvOutputFormatter` before we can test it:

```
services.AddControllers()
    .AddMvcOptions(options =>
    {
        options.RespectBrowserAcceptHeader = true;
            // false by default
        options.OutputFormatters.Add(
```

```
                new XmlSerializerOutputFormatter();

            // register the VcardOutputFormatter
            options.OutputFormatters.Add(
                new VcardOutputFormatter());
            // register the CsvOutputFormatter
            options.OutputFormatters.Add(
                new CsvOutputFormatter());
        });
```

13. In Postman, change the `Accept` header to `text/csv` and click **Send** again:

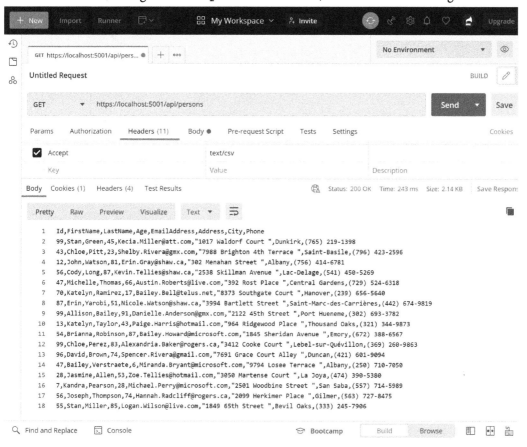

Figure 7.5 – A screenshot of text/CSV output in Postman

There we go: Postman was able to open all of the formats we tested.

Summary

Isn't that cool? The ability to change the format based on the `Accept` header is very handy. This way, you are able to create a Web API for many different clients: one that accepts many different formats, depending on the clients' preferences. There are still a lot of potential clients out there that don't use JSON and prefer XML or CSV.

The other way around would be an option to consume CSV data or any other format inside the Web API. Let's assume your client sends you a list of people in CSV format. How would you solve this? Parsing the string manually in the `action` method would work, but it's not an easy option.

This is what `ModelBinders` can do for us. Let's see how that works in the next chapter.

8
Managing Inputs with Custom ModelBinders

In the last chapter regarding `OutputFormatters`, we learned about sending data out to clients in different formats. In this chapter, we are going to do it the other way. This chapter is about data you get in your Web API from outside; for instance, what to do if you get data in a special format, or if you get data you need to validate in a special way. **ModelBinders** will help you to handle this.

In this chapter, we will be covering the following topics:

- Introducing `ModelBinders`
- Creating a custom `ModelBinder` type

The topics in this chapter refer to the **WebAPI** layer of the ASP.NET Core architecture:

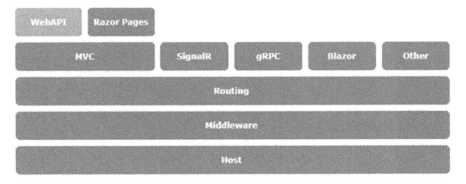

Figure 8.1 – ASP.NET Core architecture

Technical requirements

To follow the descriptions in this chapter, you will need to create an ASP.NET Core MVC application. Open your console, shell, or bash terminal, and change to your working directory. Use the following command to create a new MVC application:

```
dotnet new webapi -n ModelBinderSample -o ModelBinderSample
```

Now, open the project in Visual Studio by double-clicking the project file or, in VS Code, by typing the following command in the already open console:

```
cd ModelBinderSample
code .
```

All of the code samples in this chapter can be found in the GitHub repository for this book at https://github.com/PacktPublishing/Customizing-ASP.NET-Core-5.0/tree/main/Chapter08.

Introducing ModelBinders

ModelBinders are responsible for binding the incoming data to specific action method parameters. They bind the data sent with the request to the parameters. The default binders are able to bind data that is sent via QueryString, or sent within the request body. Within the body, the data can be sent in URL format or JSON.

The model binding tries to find the values in the request by parameter names. The form values, route data, and query string values are stored as a key-value pair collection and the binding tries to find the parameter name in the keys of the collection.

Let's demonstrate how this works with a test project.

Preparing the test data

In this section, we're going to see how to send CSV data to a Web API method. We will reuse the CSV data we created in *Chapter 7, Content Negotiation Using a Custom OutputFormatter*:

This is a snippet of the test data we want to use:

```
Id,FirstName,LastName,Age,EmailAddress,Address,City,Phone
48,Austin,Ward,49,Jake.Timms@live.com,"8814 Gravesend Neck Road
",Daly City,(620) 260-4410
2,Sierra,Smith,15,Elizabeth.Wright@hotmail.com,"1199 Marshall
Street ",Whittier,(655) 379-4362
27,Victorina,Radcliff,40,Bryce.Sanders@rogers.ca,"2663 Sutton
Street ",Bloomington,(255) 365-0521
78,Melissa,Brandzin,39,Devin.Wright@telus.net,"7439 Knight
Court ",Tool,(645) 343-2144
89,Kathryn,Perry,87,Hailey.Jenkins@hotmail.com,"5283 Vanderbilt
Street ",Carlsbad,(747) 369-4849
```

You can find the full CSV test data on GitHub at `https://github.com/ PacktPublishing/Customizing-ASP.NET-Core-5.0/blob/main/ Chapter08/testdata.csv`.

Preparing the test project

Let's prepare the project by following these steps:

1. In the already created project (refer to the *Technical requirements* section), we will now create a new empty API controller with a small action inside:

```
namespace ModelBinderSample.Controllers
{
    [Route("api/[controller]")]
    [ApiController]
    public class PersonsController : ControllerBase
```

```
    {
        public ActionResult<object> Post(
            IEnumerable<Person> persons)
        {
            return new
            {
                ItemsRead = persons.Count(),
                Persons = persons
            };
        }
    }
}
```

This looks basically like any other action. It accepts a list of persons and returns an anonymous object that contains the number of persons as well as the list of persons. This action is pretty useless but helps us to debug ModelBinders using Postman.

2. We also need the Person class:

```
[ModelBinder(BinderType = typeof(PersonsCsvBinder))]
public class Person
{
    public int Id { get; set; }
    public string FirstName { get; set; }
    public string LastName { get; set; }
    public int Age { get; set; }
    public string EmailAddress { get; set; }
    public string Address { get; set; }
    public string City { get; set; }
    public string Phone { get; set; }
}
```

This will actually work fine if we want to send JSON-based data to that action.

3. As a last preparation step, we need to add the CsvHelper NuGet package to parse the CSV data more easily. The .NET CLI is also useful here:

```
dotnet add package CsvHelper
dotnet add package System.Linq.Async
```

> **Note**
>
> The `System.Linq.Async` package is needed to handle
> `IAsyncEnumerable` that gets returned by the `GetRecordsAsync()`
> method.

Now that this is all set up, we can try it out and create `PersonsCsvBinder` in the
next section.

Creating PersonsCsvBinder

Let's build a binder.

To create `ModelBinder`, add a new class called `PersonsCsvBinder`, which
implements `IModelBinder`. In the `BindModelAsync` method, we get
`ModelBindingContext` with all the information in it that we need in order to get the
data and to deserialize it. The following code snippets show a generic binder that should
work with any list of models. We have split it into sections so that you can clearly see how
each part of the binder works:

```
public class PersonsCsvBinder : IModelBinder
{
    public async Task BindModelAsync(
        ModelBindingContext bindingContext)
    {
        if (bindingContext == null)
        {
            return;
        }

        var modelName = bindingContext.ModelName;
        if (String.IsNullOrEmpty(modelName))
        {
            modelName = bindingContext.OriginalModelName;
        }
        if (String.IsNullOrEmpty(modelName))
        {
            return;
        }
```

As you can see from the preceding code block, first, the context is checked against null. After that, we set a default argument name to the model, if none have already been specified. If this is done, we are able to fetch the value by the name we set previously:

```
var valueProviderResult =
  bindingContext.ValueProvider.GetValue(modelName);
if (valueProviderResult == ValueProviderResult.None)
{
    return;
}
```

In the next part, if there's no value, we shouldn't throw an exception in this case. The reason is that the next configured `ModelBinder` might be responsible. If we throw an exception, the execution of the current request is canceled and the next configured `ModelBinder` doesn't have the opportunity to be executed:

```
bindingContext.ModelState.SetModelValue(
    modelName, valueProviderResult);

var value = valueProviderResult.FirstValue;
// Check if the argument value is null or empty
if (String.IsNullOrEmpty(value))
{
    return;
}
```

If we have the value, we can instantiate a new `StringReader` type that needs to be passed to `CsvReader`:

```
var stringReader = new StringReader(value);
var reader = new CsvReader(
    stringReader, CultureInfo.InvariantCulture);
```

With `CsvReader`, we can deserialize the CSV string value into a list of `Persons`. If we have the list, we need to create a new, successful `ModelBindingResult` type that needs to be assigned to the `Result` property of `ModelBindingContext`:

```
        var asyncModel = reader.GetRecordsAsync<Person>();
        var model = await asyncModel.ToListAsync();
        bindingContext.Result =
            ModelBindingResult.Success(model);
    }
}
```

You might need to add the following `using` statements at the beginning of the file:

```
using Microsoft.AspNetCore.Mvc.ModelBinding;
using System.IO;
using CsvHelper
using System.Globalization;
```

Next, we'll put `ModelBinder` to work.

Using ModelBinder

The binder isn't used automatically because it isn't registered in the dependency injection container and is not configured to be used within the MVC framework.

The easiest way to use this model binder is to use `ModelBinderAttribute` on the argument of the action where the model should be bound:

```
[HttpPost]
public ActionResult<object> Post(
    [ModelBinder(binderType: typeof(PersonsCsvBinder))]
    IEnumerable<Person> persons)
{
    return new
    {
        ItemsRead = persons.Count(),
        Persons = persons
    };
}
```

Here, the type of our `PersonsCsvBinder` is set as `binderType` to that attribute.

> **Note**
> **Steve Gordon** wrote about a second option in his blog post, *Custom ModelBinding in ASP.NET MVC Core*. He uses `ModelBinderProvider` to add the `ModelBinder` to the list of existing ones.

I personally prefer the explicit declaration because most custom `ModelBinders` will be specific to an action or to a specific type, and it prevents hidden magic in the background.

Now, let's test out what we've built.

Testing ModelBinder

To test it, we need to create a new request in Postman:

1. Start the application by running `dotnet run` in the console or by pressing *F5* in Visual Studio or VS Code.

2. First, we will set the request type to **POST** and insert the URL `https://localhost:5001/api/persons` in the address bar.

3. Next, we need to add the CSV data to the body of the request. Select `form-data` as the body type, add the `persons` key, and paste the following lines in the **value** field:

```
Id,FirstName,LastName,Age,EmailAddress,Address,City,Phone
48,Austin,Ward,49,Jake.Timms@live.com,"8814 Gravesend
   Neck Road ",Daly City,(620) 260-4410
2,Sierra,Smith,15,Elizabeth.Wright@hotmail.com,"1199
   Marshall Street ",Whittier,(655) 379-4362
27,Victorina,Radcliff,40,Bryce.Sanders@rogers.ca,"2663
   Sutton Street ",Bloomington,(255) 365-0521
```

4.   After pressing **Send**, we get the result as shown in *Figure 8.2*:

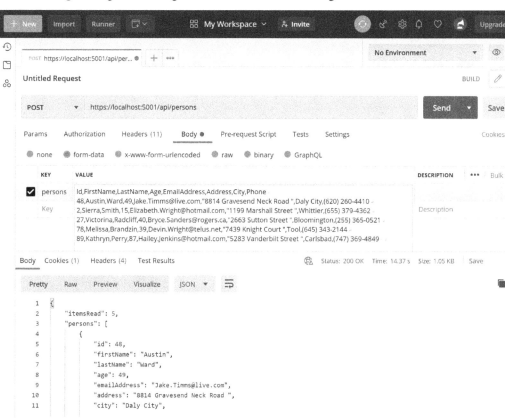

Figure 8.2 – A screenshot of CSV data in Postman

Now, the clients will be able to send CSV-based data to the server.

Summary

This is a good way to transform the input in a way that the action really needs. You could also use `ModelBinders` to do some custom validation against the database or whatever you need to do before the model gets passed to the action.

In the next chapter, we will see what you can do with `ActionFilters`.

Further reading

To learn more about `ModelBinders`, you should have a look at the following reasonably detailed documentation:

- Steve Gordon, *Custom ModelBinding in ASP.NET MVC Core*: `https://www.stevejgordon.co.uk/html-encode-string-aspnet-core-model-binding/`

- *Model Binding in ASP.NET Core*: `https://docs.microsoft.com/en-us/aspnet/core/mvc/models/model-binding`

- *Custom Model Binding in ASP.NET Core*: `https://docs.microsoft.com/en-us/aspnet/core/mvc/advanced/custom-model-binding`

9
Creating a Custom ActionFilter

We will keep on customizing at controller level in this chapter. We'll have a look into **ActionFilters** and how to create your own `ActionFilters` to keep your actions small and readable.

In this chapter, we will be covering the following topics:

- Introducing `ActionFilters`
- Using `ActionFilters`

The topics in this chapter refer to the **MVC** layer of the ASP.NET Core architecture:

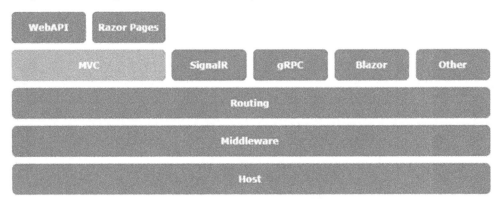

Figure 9.1 – ASP.NET Core architecture

Technical requirements

To follow the descriptions in this chapter, you will need to create an ASP.NET Core MVC application. Open your console, shell, or bash terminal, and change to your working directory. Use the following command to create a new MVC application:

```
dotnet new mvc -n ActionFilterSample -o ActionFilterSample
```

Now, open the project in Visual Studio by double-clicking the project file or, in VS Code, by typing the following command in the already-open console:

```
cd ActionFilterSample
code .
```

All of the code samples in this chapter can be found in the GitHub repository for this book at https://github.com/PacktPublishing/Customizing-ASP.NET-Core-5.0/tree/main/Chapter09.

Introducing ActionFilters

`ActionFilters` are a little bit like middleware because they can manipulate the input and the output, but are executed immediately on a specific action or on all actions of a specific controller on the MVC layer, whereas middleware works directly on the request object on the hosting layer. `ActionFilters` are created to execute code right before or after the action is executed. They are introduced to execute aspects that are not part of the actual action logic: **authorization** is one example of these aspects. `AuthorizeAttribute` is used to allow users or groups to access specific actions or controllers. The `AuthorizeAttribute` is an `ActionFilter`. It checks whether the logged-on user is authorized. If not, it redirects them to the login page.

> **Note**
>
> If you apply an `ActionFilter` globally, it executes on all actions in your application.

The following code sample shows the skeleton of a normal `ActionFilter` and an async `ActionFilter`:

```
using Microsoft.AspNetCore.Mvc.Filters;

public class SampleActionFilter : IActionFilter
{
    public void OnActionExecuting(
        ActionExecutingContext context)
    {
        // do something before the action executes
    }

    public void OnActionExecuted(
        ActionExecutedContext context)
    {
        // do something after the action executes
    }
}

public class SampleAsyncActionFilter : IAsyncActionFilter
{
```

```
public async Task OnActionExecutionAsync(
    ActionExecutingContext context,
    ActionExecutionDelegate next)
{
    // do something before the action executes

    var resultContext = await next();

    // do something after the action executes
    // resultContext.Result will be set
}
}
```

As you can see here, there are always two methods in terms of placing code to execute before and after the target action is executed. These ActionFilters cannot be used as attributes. If you want to use the ActionFilters as attributes in your controllers, you need to derive them from Attribute or from ActionFilterAttribute, as shown in the following code:

```
public class ValidateModelAttribute : ActionFilterAttribute
{
    public override void OnActionExecuting(
        ActionExecutingContext context)
    {
        if (!context.ModelState.IsValid)
        {
            context.Result = new BadRequestObjectResult(
                context.ModelState);
        }
    }
}
```

The preceding code shows a simple ActionFilter that always returns a BadRequestObjectResult if the ModelState is not valid. This may be useful within a Web API as a default check on POST, PUT, and PATCH requests. This could be extended with a lot more validation logic. We'll see how to use it later on.

Another possible use case for an `ActionFilter` is logging. You don't need to log in to the `Actions` controller directly. You can do this in an action filter to keep your actions readable with relevant code:

```csharp
using Microsoft.Extensions.Logging;

public class LoggingActionFilter : IActionFilter
{
    ILogger _logger;
    public LoggingActionFilter(ILoggerFactory loggerFactory)
    {
        _logger =
            loggerFactory.CreateLogger<LoggingActionFilter>();
    }

    public void OnActionExecuting(
        ActionExecutingContext context)
    {
        _logger.LogInformation($"Action
            '{context.ActionDescriptor.DisplayName}'
                executing");
    }

    public void OnActionExecuted(
        ActionExecutedContext context)
    {
        _logger.LogInformation($"Action
            '{context.ActionDescriptor.DisplayName}'
                executed");
    }
}
```

This logs an informational message out to the console. You can get more information regarding the current action from `ActionExecutingContext` or `ActionExecutedContext`, for example, the arguments, or the argument values. This makes the `ActionFilters` pretty useful.

Let's see how `ActionFilters` work in practice.

Using ActionFilters

ActionFilters that are actually Attributes can be registered as an attribute of an Action or a Controller, as you can see from the following demo code:

```
[HttpPost]
[ValidateModel] // ActionFilter as attribute
public ActionResult<Person> Post([FromBody] Person model)
{
    // save the person

    return model; //just to test the action
}
```

Here, we use ValidateModelAttribute, which checks ModelState and returns BadRequestObjectResult in case the ModelState is invalid; we don't need to check the ModelState in the actual action.

To register ActionFilters globally, you need to extend the MVC registration in the ConfigureServices method of Startup.cs:

```
services.AddControllersWithViews()
    .AddMvcOptions(options =>
    {
        options.Filters.Add(new SampleActionFilter());
        options.Filters.Add(new SampleAsyncActionFilter());
    });
```

ActionFilters registered in this way will be executed on every action. This way, you are able to use ActionFilters that don't derive from an Attribute.

The LoggingActionFilter type we created previously is a little more special. It is dependent on an instance of ILoggerFactory, which needs to be passed into the constructor. This won't work well as an attribute, because Attributes don't support constructor injection via dependency injection. The ILoggerFactory is registered in the ASP.NET Core dependency injection container and needs to be injected into LoggingActionFilter.

Because of this, there are some more ways to register ActionFilters. Globally, we are able to register them as a type that gets instantiated by the dependency injection container and the dependencies can be solved by the container:

```
services.AddControllersWithViews()
    .AddMvcOptions(options =>
    {
        options.Filters.Add<LoggingActionFilter>();
    })
```

This works well. We now have the ILoggerFactory in the filter.

To support automatic resolution in Attributes, you need to use ServiceFilterAttribute on the controller or action level:

```
[ServiceFilter(typeof(LoggingActionFilter))]
public class HomeController : Controller
{
```

In addition to the global filter registration, the ActionFilter needs to be registered in ServiceCollection before we can use it with ServiceFilterAttribute:

```
services.AddSingleton<LoggingActionFilter>();
```

To be complete, there is another way to use ActionFilters that requires arguments passed to the constructor. You can use TypeFilterAttribute to automatically instantiate the filter. However, in using this attribute, the filter *isn't* instantiated by the dependency injection container; the arguments need to be specified as arguments of TypeFilterAttribute.

See the following code snippet from the official documentation:

```
[TypeFilter(typeof(AddHeaderAttribute),
    Arguments = new object[] { "Author", "Juergen Gutsch
        (@sharpcms)" })]
public IActionResult Hi(string name)
{
    return Content($"Hi {name}");
}
```

The type of filter and the arguments are specified with `TypeFilterAttribute`. `AddHeaderAttribute` is one of the `ActionFilter` attributes provided by the ASP. NET Core framework.

Summary

`ActionFilters` give us an easy way to keep the actions clean. If we find repeating tasks inside our actions that are not really relevant to the actual responsibility of the action, we can move those tasks out to an `ActionFilter`, or maybe `ModelBinder` or a `MiddleWare`, depending on how globally it needs to work. The more relevant it is to an action, the more appropriate it is to use an `ActionFilter`.

There are other kinds of filters, which all work in a similar fashion. To learn more about the different kinds of filters, reading the documentation proposed is definitely recommended.

In the next chapter, we will move on to the actual view logic and extend the Razor views with custom `TagHelpers`.

Further reading

Microsoft ASP.NET Core controllers: `https://docs.microsoft.com/en-us/aspnet/core/mvc/controllers/filters`

10

Creating Custom TagHelpers

In this tenth chapter, we're going to talk about **TagHelpers**. The built-in `TagHelpers` are pretty useful and make the Razor code much prettier and more readable. Creating custom `TagHelpers` will make your life much easier.

In this chapter, we will be covering the following topics:

- Introducing `TagHelpers`
- Creating custom `TagHelpers`

The topics in this chapter refer to the **MVC** layer of the ASP.NET Core architecture:

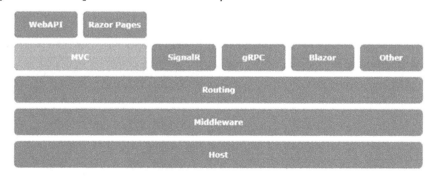

Figure 10.1 – ASP.NET Core architecture

Technical requirements

To follow the descriptions in this chapter, you will need to create an ASP.NET Core MVC application. Open your console, shell, or bash terminal, and change to your working directory. Use the following command to create a new MVC application:

```
dotnet new mvc -n TagHelperSample -o TagHelperSample
```

Now open the project in Visual Studio by double-clicking the project file or, in VS Code, by typing the following command in the already open console:

```
cd TagHelperSample
code .
```

All of the code samples in this chapter can be found in the GitHub repository for this book at `https://github.com/PacktPublishing/Customizing-ASP.NET-Core-5.0/tree/main/Chapter10`.

Introducing TagHelpers

With **TagHelpers**, you are able to extend existing HTML tags or to create new tags that get rendered on the server side. Neither the extensions nor the new tags are visible in the browsers. `TagHelpers` are a kind of shortcut to write easier (and less) HTML or Razor code on the server side. `TagHelpers` will be interpreted on the server and will produce "real" HTML code for the browsers.

`TagHelpers` are not a new thing in ASP.NET Core. They have been present since the first version of ASP.NET Core. Most existing and built-in `TagHelpers` are a replacement for the old-fashioned HTML helpers, which still exist and work in ASP.NET Core to keep the Razor views compatible with ASP.NET Core.

A very basic example of extending HTML tags is the built-in `AnchorTagHelper`:

```
<!-- old fashioned HtmlHelper -->
@Html.ActionLink("Home", "Index", "Home")
<!-- new TagHelper -->
<a asp-controller="Home" asp-action="Index">Home</a>
```

Many HTML developers find it a bit strange to have `HtmlHelper` between the HTML tags. It is hard to read, and is kind of disruptive while reading the code. Perhaps not for ASP.NET Core developers who are used to reading that kind of code, but compared to `TagHelpers`, it is really ugly. `TagHelpers` feel more natural and more like HTML, even if they are not, and even if they are getting rendered on the server.

Many `HtmlHelper` instances can be replaced with `TagHelper`.

There are also some new tags that have been built with `TagHelpers`, tags that are not in HTML, but look like HTML. One example is `EnvironmentTagHelper`:

```
<environment include="Development">
    <link rel="stylesheet"
        href="~/lib/bootstrap/dist/css/bootstrap.css" />
    <link rel="stylesheet" href="~/css/site.css" />
</environment>
<environment exclude="Development">
    <link rel="stylesheet"
        href="https://ajax.aspnetcdn.com/ajax/bootstrap/3.3.7/
            css/bootstrap.min.css"
            asp-fallback-href="~/lib/bootstrap/dist/css/
                bootstrap.min.css"
            asp-fallback-test-class="sr-only"
            asp-fallback-test-property="position"
            asp-fallback-test-value="absolute" />
    <link rel="stylesheet"
        href="~/css/site.min.css"
        asp-append-version="true" />
</environment>
```

This `TagHelper` renders (or doesn't render) the contents depending on the current runtime environment. In this case, the target environment is the development mode. The first **environment** tag renders the contents if the current runtime environment is set to `Development`, and the second one renders the contents if it is *not* set to `Development`. This makes it a useful helper in rendering debugable scripts or styles in `Development` mode and minified and optimized code in any other runtime environment.

Let's now see how we can create our own custom `TagHelpers`.

Creating custom TagHelpers

To use all the custom `TagHelpers` that we will create in this chapter, you need to refer to the current assembly to tell the framework where to find the `TagHelpers`. Open the `_ViewImports.cshtml` file in the `View/Shared/` folder and add the following line at the end of the file:

```
@addTagHelper *, TagHelperSample
```

Here's a quick example showing how to extend an existing tag using a `TagHelper`:

1. Let's assume we need to have a tag configured as bold and colored in a specific color:

    ```
    <p strong color="red">Use this area to provide
        additional information.</p>
    ```

    This looks like pretty old-fashioned HTML out of the nineties, but this is just to demonstrate a simple `TagHelper`.

2. The current method to do this task is to use a `TagHelper` to extend any tag that has an attribute called `strong`, as shown in the following code snippet:

    ```
    [HtmlTargetElement(Attributes = "strong")]
    public class StrongTagHelper : TagHelper
    {
        public string Color { get; set; }

        public override void Process(
            TagHelperContext context,
            TagHelperOutput output)
        {
            output.Attributes.RemoveAll("strong");

            output.Attributes.Add("style",
                "font-weight:bold;");
            if (!String.IsNullOrWhiteSpace(Color))
            {
                output.Attributes.RemoveAll("style");
                output.Attributes.Add("style",
                    $"font-weight:bold;color:{Color};");
    ```

```
            }
        }
    }
```

The first line tells the tag helper to work on tags with a target attribute of `strong`. This `TagHelper` doesn't define its own tag, but it does provide an additional attribute to specify the color.

The `Process` method defines how to render the HTML to the output stream. In this case, it adds some CSS inline styles to the current tag. It also removes the target attribute from the current tag. The `color` attribute won't show up.

This will appear as follows:

```
<p style="font-weight:bold;color:red;">Use this area
    to provide additional information.</p>
```

The next sample shows how to define a custom tag using a `TagHelper`:

1. Let's create this class, called `GreeterTagHelper`:

    ```
    public class GreeterTagHelper : TagHelper
    {
        [HtmlAttributeName("name")]
        public string Name { get; set; }

        public override void Process(
            TagHelperContext context,
            TagHelperOutput output)
        {
            output.TagName = "p";
            output.Content.SetContent($"Hello {Name}");
        }
    }
    ```

2. This `TagHelper` handles a `greeter` tag that has a property name. In the `Process` method, the current tag will be changed to a p tag and the new content is set as the current output:

    ```
    <greeter name="Readers"></greeter>
    ```

The result looks like this:

```
<p>Hello Readers</p>
```

But what if you need to do something a bit more complicated? Let's explore further.

Examining a more complex scenario

The `TagHelpers` in the last section were pretty basic, simply designed to show how `TagHelpers` work. The next sample is a little more complex, and shows a real scenario. This `TagHelper` renders a table with a list of items. This is a generic `TagHelper` and shows a real reason to create your own custom `TagHelpers`. With this, you are able to reuse an isolated piece of view code. For example, you can wrap **Bootstrap** components to make it much easier to use with just one tag, instead of nesting five levels of `div` tags. Alternatively, you can just simplify your Razor views:

1. Let's start by creating the `DataGridTagHelper` class. This next code snippet isn't complete, but we will complete the `DataGridTagHelper` class in the following steps:

```
public class DataGridTagHelper : TagHelper
{
    [HtmlAttributeName("Items")]
    public IEnumerable<object> Items { get; set; }

    public override void Process(
        TagHelperContext context,
        TagHelperOutput output)
    {
        output.TagName = "table";
        output.Attributes.Add("class", "table");
        var props = GetItemProperties();

        TableHeader(output, props);
        TableBody(output, props);
    }
}
```

In the `Process` method, we call private sub-methods that do the actual work to make the class a little more readable.

You might need to add the following `using` statements at the beginning of the file:

```
using System.Reflection;
using System.ComponentModel;
using System.ComponentModel;
```

2. Because this is a generic `TagHelper`, incoming objects need to be analyzed. The `GetItemProperties` method gets the type of the property items and loads `PropertyInfos` from the type. `PropertyInfos` will be used to get the table headers and the values:

```
private PropertyInfo[] GetItemProperties()
{
    var listType = Items.GetType();
    Type itemType;
    if (listType.IsGenericType)
    {
        itemType = listType.GetGenericArguments()
            .First();
        return itemType.GetProperties(
            BindingFlags.Public |
            BindingFlags.Instance);
    }
    return new PropertyInfo[] { };
}
```

3. The following code snippet shows the generation of the table headers. The `TableHeader` method writes the requisite HTML tags directly to `TagHelperOutput`. It also uses the list of `PropertyInfos` to get the property names that will be used as table header names:

```
private void TableHeader(
    TagHelperOutput output,
    PropertyInfo[] props)
{
    output.Content.AppendHtml("<thead>");
    output.Content.AppendHtml("<tr>");
    foreach (var prop in props)
    {
```

```
        var name = GetPropertyName(prop);
        output.Content.AppendHtml($"<th>{name}</th>");
    }
    output.Content.AppendHtml("</tr>");
    output.Content.AppendHtml("</thead>");
}
```

4. Using property names as table header names is not always useful. This is why the GetPropertyName method also tries to read the value from DisplayNameAttribute, which is part of DataAnnotation that is heavily used in data models that are displayed in MVC user interfaces. Therefore, it makes sense to support this attribute:

```
private string GetPropertyName(
    PropertyInfo property)
{
    var attribute = property
        .GetCustomAttribute<DisplayNameAttribute>();
    if (attribute != null)
    {
        return attribute.DisplayName;
    }
    return property.Name;
}
```

5. Also, values need to be displayed. The TableBody method does that job:

```
private void TableBody(
    TagHelperOutput output,
    PropertyInfo[] props)
{
    output.Content.AppendHtml("<tbody>");
    foreach (var item in Items)
    {
        output.Content.AppendHtml("<tr>");
        foreach (var prop in props)
        {
            var value = GetPropertyValue(prop, item);
```

```
                output.Content.AppendHtml(
                    $"<td>{value}</td>");
            }
            output.Content.AppendHtml("</tr>");
        }
        output.Content.AppendHtml("</tbody>");
    }
```

6. To get the values from the actual object, the `GetPropertyValue` method is used:

```
private object GetPropertyValue(
    PropertyInfo property,
    object instance)
{
    return property.GetValue(instance);
}
```

7. To use this `TagHelper`, you just need to assign a list of items to this tag:

```
<data-grid items="Model.Persons"></data-grid>
```

In this case, it is a list of persons, which we get in the `Persons` property of our current model.

8. The `Person` class we are using here looks like this:

```
public class Person
{
    [DisplayName("First name")]
    public string FirstName { get; set; }

    [DisplayName("Last name")]
    public string LastName { get; set; }

    public int Age { get; set; }

    [DisplayName("Email address")]
    public string EmailAddress { get; set; }
}
```

So, not all of the properties have `DisplayNameAttribute`, so the fallback in the `GetPropertyName` method is needed to get the actual property name instead of the `DisplayName` value.

9. This `TagHelper` needs some more checks and validations before you can use it in production, but it works. It displays a list of fake data that is generated using GenFu (see *Chapter 7, Content Negotiation Using a Custom OutputFormatter*, to learn about GenFu):

TagHelperSample			Home About Contact
First name	**Last name**	**Age**	**Email address**
Autumn	Gomes	11	Michelle.Tellies@gmx.com
Grace	Cox	26	Jillian.Russell@gmx.com
Angel	Gonzalez	7	Emma.Getzlaff@rogers.ca
Jackson	Daeninck	2	Timothy.Clark@hotmail.com
Jason	Sanchez	80	Erin.Morris@rogers.ca
Ashley	Turner	34	Amanda.Phillips@telus.net
Danyel	Rogers	65	Tanner.Wilson@gmx.com
Madison	Anderson	61	Tanner.Flores@microsoft.com
Emelda	Price	19	Autumn.Collins@shaw.ca
Violet	Green	37	Jennifer.Ross@rogers.ca
Chris	Scott	72	Luis.Anderson@shaw.ca
Danyel	Jackson	14	Brian.Long@shaw.ca
Jason	Powell	8	Jenna.Choi@live.com
Alyssa	Hayes	47	Rebecca.Torres@gmx.com

Figure 10.2 – The TagHelper sample in action

Now, you are able to extend this `TagHelper` with a lot more features, including sorting, filtering, and paging. Feel free to try it out in a variety of contexts.

Summary

`TagHelpers` are pretty useful when it comes to reusing parts of the view and simplifying and cleaning up your views, as in the sample regarding `DataGridTagHelper`. You can also provide a library with useful view elements. There are some more examples of pre-existing `TabHelper` libraries and samples that you can try out in the *Further reading* section.

In the next chapter, we're going to talk about how to customize the hosting of ASP.NET Core web applications.

Further reading

- Damian Edwards, *TagHelperPack*: `https://github.com/DamianEdwards/TagHelperPack`

- David Paquette, *TagHelperSamples*: `https://github.com/dpaquette/TagHelperSamples`

- *TagHelpers for Bootstrap by Teleric*: `https://www.red-gate.com/simple-talk/dotnet/asp-net/asp-net-core-tag-helpers-bootstrap/`

- *TagHelpers for jQuery*: `https://www.jqwidgets.com/asp.net-core-mvc-tag-helpers/`

11
Configuring WebHostBuilder

When reading *Chapter 4, Configuring and Customizing HTTPS with Kestrel*, you might have asked yourself, *How can I use user secrets to pass the password to the HTTPS configuration?* You might even be wondering whether you can fetch the configuration from within `Program.cs`.

In this chapter, we're going to answer this question through the following topic:

- Re-examining `WebHostBuilderContext`

The topics in this chapter refer to the **Host** layer of the ASP.NET Core architecture:

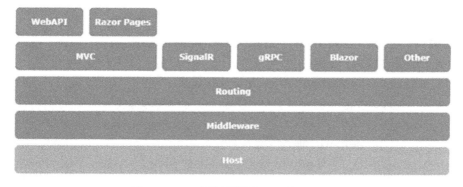

Figure 11.1 – ASP.NET Core architecture

Technical requirements

To follow the exercises in this chapter, you will need to create an ASP.NET Core application. Open your console, shell, or bash terminal, and change to your working directory. Use the following command to create a new web application:

```
dotnet new web -n HostBuilderConfig -o HostBuilderConfig
```

Now open the project in Visual Studio by double-clicking the project file or, in VS Code, by typing the following command in the already open console:

```
cd HostBuilderConfig
code .
```

All of the code samples in this chapter can be found in the GitHub repository for this book at https://github.com/PacktPublishing/Customizing-ASP. NET-Core-5.0/tree/main/Chapter11.

Re-examining WebHostBuilderContext

Remember the WebHostBuilderContext Kestrel configuration in the Program.cs that we looked at in *Chapter 4, Configuring and Customizing HTTPS with Kestrel*? In that chapter, we saw that you should use user secrets to configure the certificate's password, as shown in the following code snippet:

```
public class Program
{
    public static void Main(string[] args)
    {
        CreateHostBuilder(args).Build().Run();
    }

    public static IHostBuilder CreateHostBuilder(
        string[] args) =>
        Host.CreateDefaultBuilder(args)
            .ConfigureWebHostDefaults(webBuilder =>
            {
                webBuilder
                    .UseKestrel(options =>
                    {
```

```
                        options.Listen(
                            IPAddress.Loopback,
                            5000);
                        options.Listen(
                            IPAddress.Loopback,
                            5001,
                            listenOptions =>
                            {
                                listenOptions.UseHttps(
                                    "certificate.pfx",
                                    "topsecret");
                            });
                    })
                    .UseStartup<Startup>();
            });
    }
}
```

Usually, you are not able to fetch the configuration inside this code. You need to know that the UseKestrel() method is overloaded, as you can see here:

```
.UseKestrel((host, options) =>
{
    // ...
})
```

This first argument is a WebHostBuilderContext type, which you can use to access the configuration. So, let's rewrite the lambda a little bit to use this context:

```
.UseKestrel((host, options) =>
{
    var filename = host.Configuration.GetValue(
        "AppSettings:certfilename", "");
    var password = host.Configuration.GetValue(
        "AppSettings:certpassword", "");

    options.Listen(IPAddress.Loopback, 5000);
    options.Listen(IPAddress.Loopback, 5001,
```

```
            listenOptions =>
            {
                listenOptions.UseHttps(filename, password);
            });
    })
```

In this sample, we write the keys using the colon divider because this is the way in which you need to read nested configurations from appsettings.json:

```
{
    "AppSettings": {
        "certfilename": "certificate.pfx",
        "certpassword": "topsecret"
    },
    "Logging": {
        "LogLevel": {
            "Default": "Warning"
        }
    },
    "AllowedHosts": "*"
}
```

> **Important note**
> This is just a sample of how to read configurations to configure Kestrel. Please never, *ever* store any credentials inside the code. Use the following concepts instead.

You are also able to read from the user secrets store where the keys are set up, like this:

```
dotnet user-secrets init
dotnet user-secrets set "AppSettings:certfilename"
  "certificate.pfx"
dotnet user-secrets set "AppSettings:certpassword"
  "topsecret"
```

This also applies to environment variables:

```
SET APPSETTINGS_CERTFILENAME=certificate.pfx
SET APPSETTINGS_CERTPASSWORD=topsecret
```

> **Important note**
>
> Since the user secrets store is for local development only, you should pass credentials via environment variables to the application in production, or production-like applications. Also, the App Settings configuration you will set up in Azure will be passed as environment variables to your application.

So, how does this all work?

How does it work?

Do you remember the days back when you needed to configure app configurations in `Startup.cs` ASP.NET Core 1.0? That was configured in the constructor of the startup class and looked similar to this, if you added user secrets:

```
var builder = new ConfigurationBuilder()
    .SetBasePath(env.ContentRootPath)
    .AddJsonFile("appsettings.json")
    .AddJsonFile($"appsettings.{env.EnvironmentName}.json",
      optional: true);

if (env.IsDevelopment())
{
    builder.AddUserSecrets();
}

builder.AddEnvironmentVariables();
Configuration = builder.Build();
```

This code is now wrapped inside the `CreateDefaultBuilder` method (as you can see on GitHub; refer to the *Further reading* section for details) and looks like this:

```
builder.ConfigureAppConfiguration((hostingContext, config)
  =>
{
    var env = hostingContext.HostingEnvironment;

    config
        .AddJsonFile(
            "appsettings.json",
```

```
                optional: true,
                reloadOnChange: true)
            .AddJsonFile(
                $"appsettings.{env.EnvironmentName}.json",
                optional:  true,
                reloadOnChange: true);

    if (env.IsDevelopment())
    {
        var appAssembly = Assembly.Load(
            new AssemblyName(env.ApplicationName));
        if (appAssembly != null)
        {
            config.AddUserSecrets(appAssembly,
                optional: true);
        }
    }

    config.AddEnvironmentVariables();

    if (args != null)
    {
        config.AddCommandLine(args);
    }
})
```

It is almost the same code, and it is one of the first things that gets executed when building the `WebHost.cs` file.

It needs to be one of the first things because the Kestrel is configurable via the app configuration. You can specify ports and URLs and so on using environment variables or `appsettings.json`.

You can find these lines in `WebHost.cs`:

```
builder.UseKestrel((builderContext, options) =>
  {
    options.Configure(
        builderContext.Configuration.GetSection("Kestrel"));
})
```

This means that you are able to add these lines to `appsettings.json` to configure Kestrel endpoints:

```
"Kestrel": {
    "EndPoints": {
        "Http": {
            "Url": "http://localhost:5555"
        }
    }
}
```

Alternatively, environment variables such as these can be used to configure the endpoint:

```
SET KESTREL_ENDPOINTS_HTTP_URL=http://localhost:5555
```

Let's now recap everything we've covered in this chapter.

Summary

Inside `Program.cs`, you are able to use app configuration inside the lambdas of the configuration methods, provided you have access to the `WebHostBuilderContext`. This way, you can use all the configuration you like to configure `WebHostBuilder`.

In the next chapter, we are going to have a look at the hosting details. You will learn about different hosting models and how to host an ASP.NET Core application in different ways.

12
Using Different Hosting Models

In this chapter, we will talk about how to customize hosting in ASP.NET Core. We will look into the hosting options, different kinds of hosting, and take a quick look at hosting on IIS. This chapter is just an overview. It is possible to go into much greater detail as regards each topic, but that would fill a complete book on its own!

In this chapter, we will be covering the following topics:

- Setting up `WebHostBuilder`
- Setting up Kestrel
- Setting up HTTP.sys
- Hosting on IIS
- Using NGINX or Apache on Linux

The topics in this chapter refer to the **Host** layer of the ASP.NET Core architecture:

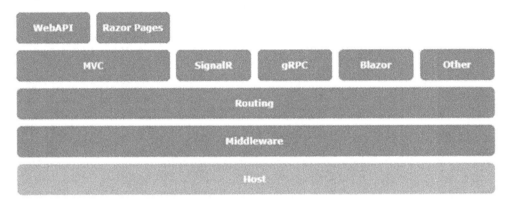

Figure 12.1 – ASP.NET Core architecture

This chapter tackles the following topics of the server architecture:

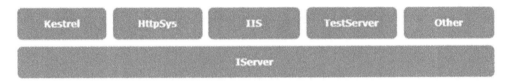

Figure 12.2 – ASP.NET server architecture

Technical requirements

For this series, we just need to set up a small empty web application:

```
dotnet new web -n ExploreHosting -o ExploreHosting
```

That's it. Open it with Visual Studio Code:

```
cd ExploreHosting
code .
```

Et voilà! A simple project opens in VS Code.

The code for this chapter can be found on GitHub here: https://github.com/PacktPublishing/Customizing-ASP.NET-Core-5.0/tree/main/Chapter12.

Setting up WebHostBuilder

As in the last chapter, we will focus on `Program.cs` in this section. `WebHostBuilder` is our friend. This is where we configure and create the web host.

The following code snippet is the default configuration of every new ASP.NET Core web we create using **File** | **New** | **Project** in Visual Studio, or running the `dotnet new` command with the .NET CLI:

```
public class Program
{
    public static void Main(string[] args)
    {
        CreateHostBuilder(args).Build().Run();
    }

    public static IWebHostBuilder CreateHostBuilder(
        string[] args) =>
        Host.CreateDefaultBuilder(args)
            .ConfigureWebHostDefaults(webBuilder =>
            {
                webBuilder.UseStartup<Startup>();
            });
}
```

As we already know from the previous chapters, the default build has all the necessary stuff pre-configured. All you require in order to run an application successfully on Azure or on an on-premises IIS is configured for you.

But you are able to override almost all of these default configurations, including the hosting configuration.

Next, let's set up Kestrel.

Setting up Kestrel

After `WebHostBuilder` is created, we can use various functions to configure the builder. Here we already see one of them, which specifies the startup class that should be used.

> **Note**
>
> As discussed in *Chapter 4, Configuring and Customizing HTTPS with Kestrel*, Kestrel is one possibility when it comes to hosting your application. Kestrel is a web server built in .NET and based on .NET socket implementations. Previously, it was built on top of `libuv`, which is the same web server that is used by Node.js. Microsoft removed the dependency on `libuv` and created their own web server implementation based on .NET Sockets.

In the last chapter, we saw the `UseKestrel` method to configure the Kestrel options:

```
.UseKestrel((host, options) =>
{
    // ...
})
```

This first argument is a `WebHostBuilderContext` type to access already configured host settings or the configuration itself. The second argument is an object to configure Kestrel. This code snippet shows what we did in the last chapter to configure the socket endpoints where the host needs to listen:

```
.UseKestrel((host, options) =>
{
    var filename = host.Configuration.GetValue(
        "AppSettings:certfilename", "");
    var password = host.Configuration.GetValue(
        "AppSettings:certpassword", "");

    options.Listen(IPAddress.Loopback, 5000);
    options.Listen(IPAddress.Loopback,  5001,
        listenOptions  =>
        {
            listenOptions.UseHttps(filename, password);
        });
})
```

This will override the default configuration where you are able to pass in URLs; for example, using the `applicationUrl` property of `launchSettings.json` or an environment variable.

Let's now look at how to set up `HTTP.sys`.

Setting up HTTP.sys

There is another hosting option; a different web server implementation. `HTTP.sys` is a pretty mature library, deep within Windows, that can be used to host your ASP.NET Core application:

```
.UseHttpSys(options =>
{
    // ...
})
```

`HTTP.sys` is different to Kestrel. It cannot be used in IIS because it is not compatible with the ASP.NET Core module for IIS.

The main reason for using `HTTP.sys` instead of Kestrel is **Windows Authentication**, which cannot be used in Kestrel. You can also use `HTTP.sys` if you need to expose your application to the internet without IIS.

> **Note**
>
> IIS has been running on top of `HTTP.sys` for years. This means that `UseHttpSys()` and IIS use the same web server implementation. To learn more about `HTTP.sys`, please read the documentation, links to which can be found in the *Further reading* section.

Next, let's look at using IIS for hosting.

Hosting on IIS

An ASP.NET Core application shouldn't be directly exposed to the internet, even if it's supported for even Kestrel or `HTTP.sys`. It would be best to have something like a reverse proxy in between, or at least a service that watches the hosting process. For ASP.NET Core, IIS isn't just a reverse proxy. It also takes care of the hosting process, in case it breaks because of an error. If that happens, IIS will restart the process. NGINX may be used as a reverse proxy on Linux that also takes care of the hosting process.

To host an ASP.NET Core web on IIS or on Azure, you need to publish it first. Publishing doesn't only compile the project; it also prepares the project for hosting on IIS, on Azure, or on a web server on Linux, such as NGINX.

The following command will publish the project:

```
dotnet publish -o ..\published -r win-x64
```

When viewed in a system browser, this should look as follows:

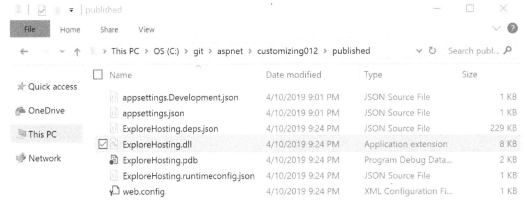

Figure 12.3 – A .NET published folder

This produces an output that can be mapped in IIS. It also creates a `web.config` file to add settings for IIS or Azure. It contains the compiled web application as a DLL.

If you publish a self-contained application, it also contains the runtime itself. A self-contained application brings its own .NET Core runtime, but the size of the delivery increases a lot.

And in IIS? Just create a new web in IIS and map it to the folder where you placed the published output:

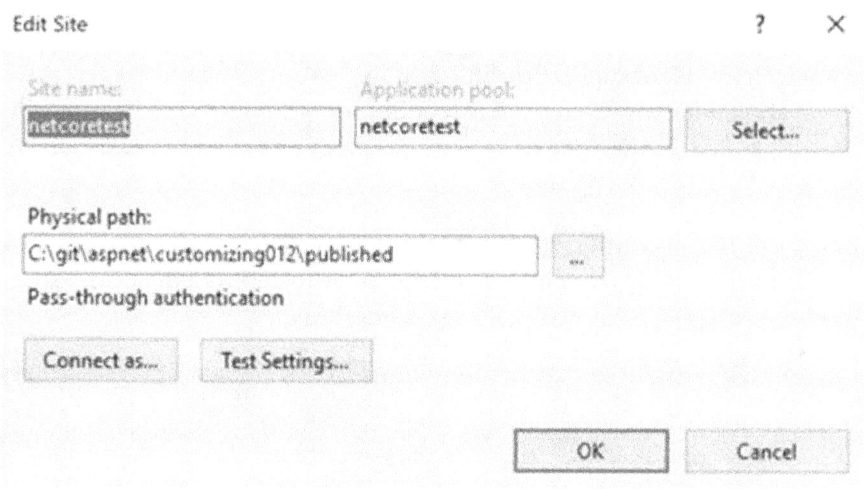

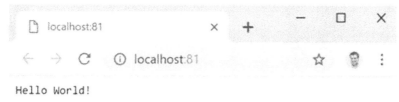

Figure 12.4 – The .NET publishing dialog

It gets a little more complicated if you need to change the security, if you have some database connections, and so on. This could be a topic for a separate chapter on its own. Here's a quick version of it though:

Hello World!

Figure 12.5 – Hello World! viewed in a browser

Figure 12.5 is the output of the small middleware in `startup.cs` of the demo project:

```
app.Run(async (context) =>
{
    await context.Response.WriteAsync("Hello World!");
});
```

Next up, we'll discuss some alternatives for Linux.

Using NGINX or Apache on Linux

Publishing an ASP.NET Core application on Linux looks very similar to the way it looks on IIS, but preparing it for the reverse proxy requires some additional steps. You will need a web server such as **NGINX** or **Apache** as a reverse proxy that forwards the traffic to Kestrel and the ASP.NET Core application:

1. First, you need to allow your app to accept two specific forwarded headers. To do this, open the `Startup.cs` file and add the following lines to the `Configure` method before the `UseAuthentication` middleware:

    ```
    app.UseForwardedHeaders(new ForwardedHeadersOptions
    {
        ForwardedHeaders = ForwardedHeaders.XForwardedFor
            | ForwardedHeaders.XForwardedProto
    });
    ```

    You also need to trust the incoming traffic from the reverse proxy. This requires you to add the following lines to the `ConfigureServices` method:

    ```
    services.Configure<ForwardedHeadersOptions>(options =>
    {
        options.KnownProxies.Add(
            IPAddress.Parse("10.0.0.100"));
    });
    ```

    Add the IP address of the proxy here. This is just a sample.

2. Then, you need to publish the application:

    ```
    dotnet publish --configuration Release
    ```

    Copy the build output to a folder called `/var/www/yourapplication`. You should also do a quick test on Linux by calling the following command:

    ```
    dotnet <yourapplication.dll>
    ```

    Here, `yourapplication.dll` is the compiled application, including the path. If it is all working correctly, you should be able to call your web on `http://localhost:5000/`.

3. If it is working, the application should run as a service. This requires you to create a service file on /etc/systemd/system/. Call the file kestrel-yourapplication.service and place the following content in it:

```
[Unit]
Description=Example .NET Web API App running on Ubuntu

[Service]
WorkingDirectory=/var/www/yourapplication
ExecStart=/usr/bin/dotnet /var/www/yourapplication/
yourapplication.dll
Restart=always

# Restart service after 10 seconds if the dotnet service
  # crashes:
RestartSec=10
KillSignal=SIGINT
SyslogIdentifier=dotnet-example
User=www-data
Environment=ASPNETCORE_ENVIRONMENT=Production
Environment=DOTNET_PRINT_TELEMETRY_MESSAGE=false

[Install]
WantedBy=multi-user.target
```

Ensure that the paths in lines 5 and 6 point to the folder where you placed the build output. This file defines that your app should run as a service on the default port. It also watches the app and restarts it in case it crashes. It also defines environment variables that get passed in to configure your application. See *Chapter 1, Customizing Logging*, to learn how to configure your application using environment variables.

Next up, we'll see how to configure NGINX.

Configuring NGINX

Now you can tell NGINX what to do using the following code:

```
server {
    listen          80;
    server_name    example.com *.example.com;
    location / {
        proxy_pass              http://localhost:5000;
        proxy_http_version 1.1;
        proxy_set_header    Upgrade $http_upgrade;
        proxy_set_header    Connection keep-alive;
        proxy_set_header    Host $host;
        proxy_cache_bypass $http_upgrade;
        proxy_set_header    X-Forwarded-For
          $proxy_add_x_forwarded_for;
        proxy_set_header    X-Forwarded-Proto $scheme;
    }
}
```

This tells NGINX to forward calls on port 80 to example.com, and subdomains of it to http://localhost:5000, which is the default address of your application.

Configuring Apache

The Apache configuration looks pretty similar to the NGINX method, and does the same things at the end:

```
<VirtualHost *:*>
    RequestHeader set "X-Forwarded-Proto" expr=%{REQUEST_
      SCHEME}
</VirtualHost>

<VirtualHost *:80>
    ProxyPreserveHost On
    ProxyPass / http://127.0.0.1:5000/
    ProxyPassReverse / http://127.0.0.1:5000/
    ServerName www.example.com
    ServerAlias *.example.com
```

```
    ErrorLog ${APACHE_LOG_DIR}yourapplication-error.log
    CustomLog ${APACHE_LOG_DIR}yourapplication-access.log
      common
  </VirtualHost>
```

That's it for NGINX and Apache. Let's now wrap up this chapter.

Summary

ASP.NET Core and the .NET CLI already contain all the tools to get up and running on various platforms and to set it up to get it ready for Azure and IIS, as well as NGINX. This is super easy, and well described in the documentation.

Currently, we have `WebHostBuilder` that creates the hosting environment of the applications. In version 3.0, we have `HostBuilder`, which is able to create a hosting environment that is completely independent from any web context.

In the final chapter of the book, we will have a look into the new endpoint routing that allows you to create your own hosted endpoints in an easy and flexible manner.

Further reading

- **Kestrel documentation**: `https://docs.microsoft.com/en-us/aspnet/core/fundamentals/servers/kestrel`

- **HTTP.sys documentation**: `https://docs.microsoft.com/en-us/aspnet/core/fundamentals/servers/httpsys?view=aspnetcore-5.0`

- **ASP.NET Core**: `https://docs.microsoft.com/en-us/aspnet/core/host-and-deploy/aspnet-core-module?view=aspnetcore-2.2`

13
Working with Endpoint Routing

In this chapter, we will talk about the new endpoint routing in ASP.NET Core. We will learn what endpoint routing is, how it works, where it is used, and how you are able to create your own routes to your own endpoints.

In this chapter, we will be covering the following topics:

- Exploring endpoint routing
- Creating custom endpoints
- Creating a more complex endpoint

The topics in this chapter refer to the **Routing** layer of the ASP.NET Core architecture:

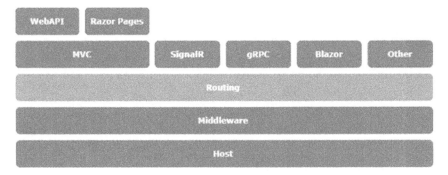

Figure 13.1 – ASP.NET Core architecture

Technical requirements

For this series, we just need to set up a small empty web application:

```
dotnet new mvc -n RoutingSample -o RoutingSample
```

That's it! Open it with Visual Studio Code:

```
cd RoutingSample
code .
```

All of the code samples in this chapter can be found in the GitHub repository for this book at https://github.com/PacktPublishing/Customizing-ASP.NET-Core-5.0/tree/main/Chapter13.

Exploring endpoint routing

To learn about **endpoint routing**, you need to learn what an endpoint is and what routing is.

The **endpoints** are the parts of the app that get executed when a route maps the incoming request to it. Let's analyze this definition in a little more detail.

A client usually requests a resource from a server. In most cases, the client is a browser. The resource is defined by a URL, which points to a specific target. In most cases, the target is a web page. It could also be a mobile app that requests specific data from a JSON Web API. What data the app requests is defined in the URL.

This means that the incoming request is also defined by the URL. The executing endpoint, on the other hand, is mapped to a specific route. A route is a URL or a pattern for a URL. ASP.NET Core developers are already familiar with such a route pattern:

```
app.UseRouting();
app.UseAuthorization();
app.UseEndpoints(endpoints =>
{
    endpoints.MapControllerRoute(
        name: "default",
        pattern: "{controller=Home}/{action=Index}/{id?}");
});
```

If the route or the route pattern matches the URL of the incoming request, the request gets mapped to that endpoint. In this case, the request gets mapped to the MVC endpoint.

ASP.NET Core can map to the following endpoints:

- Controllers (MVC, Web API)
- Razor Pages
- SignalR (and Blazor Server)
- gRPC services
- Health checks

Most of the endpoints have really simple route patterns. Only the MVC and Web API use the more complex patterns. The route definitions of Razor Pages are based on the folder and file structure of the actual pages.

Before endpoints were introduced in ASP.NET Core 2.2, routing was only a thing in MVC and Web API. The implicit routing in Razor Pages was built in there, and SignalR wasn't really ready. Blazor and gRPC weren't a thing back then and the health checks were initially implemented as a middleware.

Endpoint routing was introduced to separate routing from the actual endpoints. This makes the framework much more flexible, and new endpoints don't need to implement their own kind of routing. This way, the endpoints can use the existing flexible routing technology to get mapped to a specific route.

Next, we'll see how you can create your own custom endpoints.

Creating custom endpoints

The easiest way to create an endpoint is by using the lambda-based endpoints:

```
endpoints.Map("/map", async context =>
{
    await context.Response.WriteAsync("OK");
});
```

This maps the /map route to a simple endpoint that writes the word "OK" to the response stream.

You might need to add the Microsoft.AspNetCore.Http namespace to the using statements.

You can also map specific HTTP methods (such as GET, POST, PUT, and DELETE) to an endpoint. The following code shows how to map the GET and POST methods:

```
endpoints.MapGet("/mapget", async context =>
{
    await context.Response.WriteAsync("Map GET");
});
endpoints.MapPost("/mappost", async context =>
{
    await context.Response.WriteAsync("Map POST");
});
```

We can also map two or more HTTP methods to an endpoint:

```
endpoints.MapMethods(
    "/mapmethods",
    new[] { "DELETE", "PUT" },
    async context =>
{
    await context.Response.WriteAsync("Map Methods");
});
```

These endpoints look like the lambda-based terminating middlewares that we saw in *Chapter 6*, *Writing Custom Middleware*. Those are middlewares that terminate the pipeline and return a result, such as HTML-based views, JSON structured data, or similar. Endpoint routing is a more flexible way to create an output and should be used in all versions from ASP.NET Core 3.0 onward.

What is the benefit of using routing instead of the classical way of using `app.Map`?

In *Chapter 6*, *Writing Custom Middleware*, we saw that we can branch pipelines like this:

```
app.Map("/map1", mapped =>
{
    // some more Middlewares
});
```

This also creates a route, but this will only listen to URLs that start with `/map`. If you would prefer to have a routing engine that handles patterns such as `/map/{id:int?}` to also match `/map/456` and not `/map/abc`, you should use the new routing, as demonstrated earlier in this section.

Those lambda-based endpoints are useful for simple scenarios only. Because they are defined in `Startup.cs`, things will quickly become messy if you start to implement more complex scenarios.

We should try to find a more structured way to create custom endpoints.

Creating a more complex endpoint

In this section, we will create a more complex endpoint, step by step. Let's do this by writing a really simple health check endpoint, as you might need if you were to run your application inside a Kubernetes cluster, or just to tell others about your health status:

1. Microsoft proposes starting with the definition of the API to add the endpoint from the developer point of view. We do the same here. This means that we will add a `MapSomething` method first, without an actual implementation. This will be an extension method on `IEndpointRouteBuilder`. We are going to call it `MapMyHealthChecks`:

    ```
    // the new endpoint
    endpoints.MapMyHealthChecks("/myhealth");

    endpoints.MapControllerRoute(
    ```

```
        name: "default",
        pattern:
            "{controller=Home}/{action=Index}/{id?}");
```

The new endpoint should be added in the same way as the prebuilt endpoints, so as not to confuse any developers who need to use it.

Now that we know how the method should look, let's implement it.

2. We need to create a new static class called `MyHealthChecksExtensions` and place an extension method inside `MapMyHealthChecks`, which extends `IEndpointRouteBuilder` and returns `IEndpointConventionBuilder`:

```
public static class MapMyHealthChecksExtensions
{
    public static IEndpointConventionBuilder
      MapMyHealthChecks (
        this IEndpointRouteBuilder endpoints,
        string pattern = "/myhealth")
    {
        // ...
    }
}
```

This is just the skeleton. Let's start with the actual endpoint first before using it.

3. The actual endpoint will be written as a terminating middleware, which is a middleware that doesn't call the next one (see *Chapter 6, Writing Custom Middleware*) and creates an output to the response stream:

```
public class MyHealthChecksMiddleware
{
    private readonly ILogger<MyHealthChecksMiddleware>
      _logger;

    public MyHealthChecksMiddleware (
        RequestDelegate next,
        ILogger<MyHealthChecksMiddleware> logger)
    {
        _logger = logger;
```

```
        }

    public async Task Invoke(HttpContext context)
    {
        // add some checks here...

        context.Response.StatusCode = 200;
        context.Response.ContentType = "text/plain";
        await context.Response.WriteAsync("OK");
    }
}
```

The actual work is done in the `Invoke` method. Currently, this doesn't really do more than respond with a plaintext `OK` and the HTTP status `200`, which is fine if you just want to show that your application is running. Feel free to extend the method with actual checks, such as checking for the availability of a database, or related services, for example. Then you would need to change the HTTP status and the output related to the result of your checks.

Let's use this terminating middleware.

4. Let's go back to the skeleton of the `MapMyHealthChecks` method. We now need to create our own pipeline that we map to a given route. Place the following lines in that method:

```
var pipeline = endpoints
    .CreateApplicationBuilder()
    .UseMiddleware<MyHealthChecksMiddleware>()
    .Build();

return endpoints.Map(pattern, pipeline)
    .WithDisplayName("My custom health checks");
```

5. This approach allows you to add some more middleware just for this new pipeline. The `WithDisplayName` extension method sets the configured display name to the endpoint.

6. That's it! Press *F5* in your IDE to start the application and call `https://localhost:5001/myhealth` in your browser. You should see **OK** in your browser:

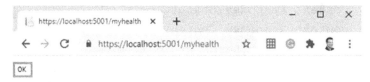

Figure 13.2 – A screenshot of the endpoint routing output

You can also convert an already existing terminating middleware to a routed endpoint to benefit from the much more flexible routing.

And that's it for this chapter!

Summary

ASP.NET Core knows many ways with which to work with a request and to provide information to the requesting client. Endpoint routing is a way to provide resources based on the requested URL and the requested method.

In this chapter, you learned how to use a terminating middleware as an endpoint that gets mapped to the new routing engine to be more flexible, matching the routes by which you want to serve the information to the requesting client.

This chapter is the last one of the book. I hope that the thirteen scenarios and recipes to customize the ASP.NET Core framework will help you to improve your applications and to get more out of ASP.NET Core.

Finally, I would also like to say thank you for reading the book!

Other Books You May Enjoy

If you enjoyed this book, you may be interested in these other titles from Packt:

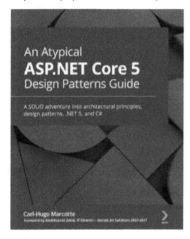

An Atypical ASP.NET Core 5 Design Patterns Guide

Carl-Hugo Marcotte

ISBN: 978-1-78934-609-1

- Apply the SOLID principles for building flexible and maintainable software
- Get to grips with .NET 5 dependency injection
- Work with GoF design patterns, such as strategy, decorator, and composite
- Explore the MVC patterns for designing web APIs and web applications using Razor
- Become familiar with CQRS and vertical slice architecture as an alternative to layering
- Understand microservices, what they are, and what they are not
- Build an ASP.NET UI from server-side to client-side Blazor

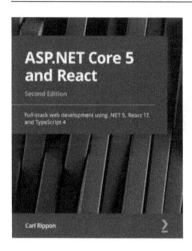

ASP.NET Core 5 and React, Second Edition

Carl Rippon

ISBN: 978-1-80020-616-8

- Build RESTful APIs with .NET 5 using API controllers

- Secure REST APIs with identity and authorization policies

- Create strongly typed, interactive, and function-based React components using Hooks

- Understand how to style React components using Emotion.js

- Perform client-side state management with Redux

- Run a range of automated tests on the frontend and backend

- Implement continuous integration and continuous delivery (CI/CD) processes in Azure using Azure DevOps

Leave a review – let other readers know what you think

Please share your thoughts on this book with others by leaving a review on the site that you bought it from. If you purchased the book from Amazon, please leave us an honest review on this book's Amazon page. This is vital so that other potential readers can see and use your unbiased opinion to make purchasing decisions, we can understand what our customers think about our products, and our authors can see your feedback on the title that they have worked with Packt to create. It will only take a few minutes of your time, but is valuable to other potential customers, our authors, and Packt. Thank you!

Index

Symbols

/map
  pipeline, branching with 62, 63

A

ActionFilters
  about 99-101
  using 102, 104
Apache
  configuring 134
  using, on Linux 132, 133
application configuration
  about 24-26
  INI files, using 28, 29
ASP.NET Core 3.0
  middleware, using on 65, 66
ASP.NET Core 5.0
  Map methods for 66

B

BackgroundService 50-52

C

configuration provider 29, 30
ConfigureContainer
  used, for registering dependencies 36
ConfigureServices method 33, 34
content negotiations 73
CSV test data, on GitHub
  reference link 89
custom logger
  creating 16-19
custom middleware
  writing 60-62
custom OutputFormatters
  creating 78-85
custom TagHelpers
  creating 108, 109
custom TagHelpers, complex scenario
  examining 110-114

D

dependency injection container
  using 32

www.ingramcontent.com/pod-product-compliance
Lightning Source LLC
Chambersburg PA
CBHW060144060326
40690CB00018B/3969